Keeping
the Heart

Keeping the Heart

How to maintain your love for God

JOHN FLAVEL

INTRODUCTION BY J. I. PACKER

TRUTHFORLIFE

CHRISTIAN HERITAGE

Scripture quotations are taken from the *King James Version*.

Introduction © J. I. Packer 2012

© Christian Focus Publications, Ltd.

ISBN 978-1-84550-648-3

Published in 1999, reprinted in 2012 and 2014
by
Christian Focus Publications
Geanies House, Fearn,
Ross-shire, IV20 1TW, Great Britain

Cover design
by
Paul Lewis

Printed in the U.S.A.

CONTENTS

INTRODUCTION

I

'Heart-work and heaven-work' was Richard Baxter's crisp characterisation of real Christianity. John Flavel, with just about every other Puritan teacher, would be in total agreement. Real Christianity has in the past been conceived in terms of orthodoxy, orthopraxy, churchmanship, sacramentalism, syncretism, and various other things, but the Puritans as a body defined it precisely in terms of communion with God – more precisely still, communion with the triune Lord through Jesus Christ the Mediator. That is what the two phrases in Baxter's definition are pointing to. 'Heaven-work' signified a discipline of which Baxter himself was the supreme promoter, namely the practice of daily motivational meditation on the prospect of finally being with Christ in heaven. The purpose of this discipline was to keep the energy level of one's discipleship as high as possible, as one continued living the forward-tilted life (so we may fairly describe it) with the eyes of one's heart fixed on the ultimate destination. 'Heart-work' was a tag term for the admonitory thought and repeated self-search that were constantly needed to sustain the most ardent love and devotion to Christ, and the firmest resistance to the many kinds of hostility and discouragement that in God's providence the Puritans had to face. John Flavel's *Keeping the Heart* (first published as *A Saint Indeed*) displays this finely, as we shall soon see.

What is the heart that Flavel, like Baxter, is talking about? The Puritan understanding of the heart is rooted, not in medical physiology, which knows the heart as a pump sending blood round the body, but in biblical theology and anthropology, which sees the heart as the central, dynamic core of personal life. The Bible uses the word in this way about a thousand times, and thereby highlights, illustrates and enforces the following truths:

(1) The human heart is the controlling source of all that we do in expression of what we are: all our thoughts, desires, discernments and decisions, our plans and purposes, our affections, attitudes and ambitions, all the wisdom and all the folly that mark our lives, come out of, and are fuelled, serviced and driven by, our hearts, for better or for worse. Our Lord Jesus showed Himself vividly aware of this. 'How can you speak good, when you are evil? For out of the abundance of the heart the mouth speaks' (Matt. 12:34). 'From within, out of the heart of man, come evil thoughts, sexual immorality, theft, murder, adultery, coveting, wickedness, deceit, sensuality, envy, slander, pride, foolishness. All these evil things come from within, and they defile a person' (Mark 7:21-23).

(2) The salvation that God gives us in Christ is rooted in a created and creative change of heart, as described by Ezekiel in an oracle about the restoring of Israel following the captivity: 'I will give you a new heart, and a new spirit

I will put within you. And I will remove the heart of stone from your flesh and give you a heart of flesh. And I will put my Spirit within you, and cause you to walk in my statutes and be careful to obey my rules' (Ezek. 36:26-27). The new, renewed heart becomes, on the one hand, the source of faith in Christ and in the gospel promises, whereby we enter a new relationship of acceptance with God; and, on the other hand, the source of love to God and man – the grateful, responsive, resolute purpose of honouring and pleasing God in all things, and seeking the best for our nearest and dearest and whoever else may cross our path. The new heart, acting in these ways, is in fact the sign of our salvation, and the inward discipline of sustaining such action is the reality of 'heart-work:' which, be it soberly said, is work indeed.

Saying this brings us to John Flavel and the book I am introducing. But before we look at the book, something should be said about the man himself.

II

A native of Bromsgrove in Worcestershire, Flavel was a preacher's son, and it does not appear that he ever wanted to be anything but a pastoral preacher himself. Born in 1628, he graduated from Oxford and became a pastor in 1650. The ministry for which he is remembered was located in Dartmouth, Devon, the port town to which he moved in 1656. He gained distinction as a preacher of the classic Puritan type, expository, analytical, didactic, applicatory, searching, converting and edifying, with divine unction regularly empowering his pulpit work. His writings reveal him as clear-headed and eloquent in the plain Puritan style, orthodox, Christ-focused and life-centred in his subject-matter, with his mind always set on advancing true godliness, with peace and joy in the Lord. It is recorded of him that he spent much time in meditation, self-examination and prayer, and on one occasion at least he had an extraordinary experience of God. Meditating on horseback, 'his thoughts began to swell and rise higher and higher like the waters in Ezekiel's vision till at last they became an overflowing flood. Such was the intention of his mind, such the ravishing tastes of heavenly joys, and such the full assurance of his interest therein, that he utterly lost a sight and sense of this world and all the concerns thereof, and for some hours he knew no more where he was than if he had been in a deep sleep upon his bed.' Stopping, exhausted, at a wayside pool, 'he sat down and washed, earnestly desiring, if it were God's pleasure, that it might be his parting place from this world. Death had the most amiable face in his eye that ever he beheld, except the face of Jesus Christ which made it so, and he could not remember, though he believed himself dying, that he had one thought of his dear wife and children or any other earthly concernment.' When he finally reached the inn to which he was heading, the innkeeper said to him, 'Sir, what is the matter with you? You look like a dead man' – to which Flavel replied, 'I was never better in my life.' At the inn, 'the influence still continued, banishing sleep. Still, still the joy of the Lord overflowed him, and he seemed to be an inhabitant of the other world. He many years after called that day one of the days of heaven.' One thinks of Paul, caught up to what he called the third heaven, and of Jonathan Edwards weeping as he walked through the woods by reason of the vividness with which he perceived the glory and beauty of God. Well may we pause in awe for a moment before moving on.

Flavel was ejected from his pulpit in 1662 as a nonconformist, following the re-establishment of the Church of England by the Act of Uniformity which itself followed the restoration of the monarchy in 1660. His people pressed him to continue his (now illegal) ministry to them, and this for two decades he did, preaching in private houses, in woodlands, on a rocky island in the Salcombe River estuary that was submerged at high tide, and in other places where the long arm of the law could be evaded. Then from 1682 to 1685 he joined with a Congregational church in London, assisting his friend William Jenkyn, commentator on Jude, who was its minister. Here, too, dodging arrest by the authorities (posses of soldiers sent out by the magistrates) was part of his way of life. When in 1687 James II lifted restrictions on nonconformist ministry, Flavel was already back in Dartmouth, and his still-loyal congregation at once erected a large church building in which his ministry could continue. He died in 1691, leaving a written legacy of biblical and devotional exposition that was first published as two large folios and that became 3,600 pages in six volumes in its 1968 reprint.

III

In *Keeping the Heart*, Flavel leads us into what, for him, is the most basic of all the disciplines of the Christian's inner life – basic to worship and prayer; basic to faith, hope and love; basic to humility, peace and joy; basic to pure-heartedness and steady obedience. What discipline is this? It is the discipline that we may call *admonitory meditation*, that is, the deployment within one's own mind of key lines of thought that will confirm and reinforce the various aspects of faithful communion with God, and recall us to Him in renewed loyalty when we have slipped away, or been drawn away, from the path of faithfulness. Such slippages begin in the mind, and begin with the contemplation of actual or potential disorder, moral or circumstantial, without relating the matter to God, and the practice of *admonitory meditation* is, in effect, talking to oneself before the Lord, reminding oneself of truths about the ways of God and the grace of Christ that will energise and stabilise one for a return to, and continuance on, the path of faithfulness, no matter what. These truths, re-anchored in the heart by applicatory meditation, will stir believers to renew their prayers for strength to carry on through thick and thin. Flavel is vividly aware that sin and Satan are constantly alluring us to follow the gleam of unthinking blind desire, and he knows how vitally important it is to counter the away-from-God thoughts and moods that lay hold of us in a way that if not checked will ruin us. Most of *Keeping the Heart* is taken up with setting out the best lines of thought with which to sustain ourselves when thus tempted in life's various ups and downs.

Would I be wrong, I wonder, to guess that most of us nowadays do very little of this thoughtful inward arguing with ourselves in times of testing? We expect that when inward or outward circumstances expose us to temptation we shall recognise it straight away and be able to banish it with a simple 'no'. But in fact keeping the heart steady, zealous for God's glory and consciously close to Christ is not always so easily done, while our expectation that we shall be able to say 'no' when necessary without inward effort and struggle only shows how unrealistic we are, and how easily we are betrayed into doing wrong and foolish things believing them to be wise and right; how easily, too, we lapse into what T.S. Eliot called 'the ultimate treason: to do the right thing for the wrong reason'. Flavel makes it evident that for him there are no shortcuts here, and that blithe self-reliance in times of testing is the high road to spiritual suicide. May we absorb His wisdom as we sit at His feet.

J.I. Packer

INTRODUCTION

*Keep thy heart with all diligence; for out of
it are the issues of life (Prov. 4:23).*

The heart of man is his worst part before it is regenerated,
and the best afterward; it is the seat of principles, and the
foundation of actions. The eye of God is, and the eye of the
Christian ought to be, principally fixed upon it.

The greatest difficulty in conversion is to win the heart *to*
God; and the greatest difficulty after conversion, is to keep
the heart *with* God. Here lies the very force and stress of
religion; here is that which makes the way to life a narrow
way, and the gate to heaven a strait gate. Direction and help
in this great work are the scope of the text: wherein we have:

1. An exhortation, 'Keep thy heart with all diligence.'

2. The reason or motive enforcing it, 'For out of it are the
    issues of life.'

In the exhortation I shall consider,

> *First,* The matter of the duty.
> *Secondly,* The manner of performing it.

1. The matter of the duty: *Keep thy heart*. Heart is not here taken properly for the noble part of the body, which philosophers call, 'the first that lives and the last that dies'; but by heart, in a metaphor, the Scripture sometimes represents some particular noble faculty of the soul. In Romans 1:21, it is put for the *understanding*: *their foolish heart*, that is, their foolish understanding *was darkened*. Psalm 119:11, it is put for the memory: 'Thy word have I hid in my heart'; and 1 John 3:20, it is put for the conscience, which includes both the light of the understanding and the recognitions of the memory; *if our heart condemn us*, that is, *if our conscience*, whose proper office it is to condemn.

But in the text we are to take it more generally, for the whole soul, or inner man. What the heart is to the body, that the soul is to the man; and what health is to the heart, that holiness is to the soul. The state of the whole body depends upon the soundness and vigour of the heart, and the everlasting state of the whole man upon the good or ill condition of the soul.

By keeping the heart, understand the *diligent* and *constant*[1] use of all holy means to preserve the soul from sin, and maintain its sweet and free communion with God. Lavater, commenting on the text, will have the word taken from a besieged garrison, beset by many enemies without, and in danger of being betrayed by treacherous citizens within, in which danger the soldiers, upon pain of death, are commanded to watch; and though the expression, *Keep thy heart*, seems to put it upon us as our work, yet it does

---

1 I say constant, for the reason added in the text extends the duty to all the states and conditions of a Christian's life, and makes it binding always. If the heart must be kept, because out of it are the issues of life, then as long as these issues of life do flow out of it, we are obliged to keep it.

not imply a sufficiency in us to do it. We are able to stop the sun in its course, or to make the rivers run backward, as by our own skill and power to rule and order our hearts. We may as well be our own *saviours* as our own *keepers;* and yet Solomon speaks properly enough when he says, *Keep thy heart,* because the duty is ours, though the power is of God; what power we have depends upon the exciting and assisting strength of Christ. Grace within us is beholden to grace without us. 'Without me ye can do nothing.' So much for the matter of the duty.

2. The manner of performing it is *with all diligence.* The Hebrew is very emphatical; *keep with all keeping,* or, *keep, keep,* set double guards. This vehemency of expression with which the duty is urged, plainly implies how difficult it is to keep our hearts, how dangerous to neglect them!

The motive to this duty is very forcible and weighty: 'For out of the heart are the issues of life.' That is, the heart is the source of all vital operations; it is the spring and original of both good and evil, as the spring in a watch that sets all the wheels in motion. The heart is the treasury, the hand and tongue but the shops; what is in these, comes from that; the hand and tongue always begin where the heart ends. The heart contrives, and the members execute: 'a good man, out of the good treasure of his heart, bringeth forth that which is good; and an evil man, out of the evil treasure of his heart, bringeth forth that which is evil: for out of the abundance of the heart his mouth speaketh.' So then, if the heart err in its work, these must miscarry in theirs; for heart errors are like the errors of the first concoction, which cannot be rectified afterward; or like the misplacing and inverting of the stamps and letters in the press, which must cause so many errata in all the copies that are printed. O then how important a duty is that which is contained in the following proposition: *The keeping and right managing of the heart in every condition, is one great business of a Christian's life.*

What the philosopher says of waters, is as properly applicable to hearts; it is hard to keep them within any bounds. God has set limits to them, yet how frequently do they transgress not only the bounds of grace and religion, but even of reason and common honesty? This is that which affords the Christian matter of labour and watchfulness, to his dying day. It is not the cleaning of the *hand* that *makes* the Christian, for many a hypocrite can show as fair a hand as he; but the purifying, watching, and right ordering of the *heart;* this is the thing that provokes so many sad complaints, and costs so many deep groans and tears. It was the pride of Hezekiah's heart that made him lie in the dust, mourning before the Lord. It was the fear of hypocrisy invading the heart that made David cry, 'Let my heart be sound in thy statutes, that I be not ashamed.' It was the sad experience he had of the divisions and distractions of his own heart in the service of God, that made him pour out the prayer, 'Unite my heart to fear thy name.'

The method in which I propose to improve the proposition is this:

First, I shall inquire what the keeping of the heart supposes and imports.

Secondly, Assign divers reasons why Christians must make this a leading business of their lives.

Thirdly, Point out those seasons which especially call for this diligence in keeping the heart.

Fourthly, Apply the whole.

1

What the Keeping of the Heart Supposes and Imports

To keep the heart, necessarily supposes a previous work of regeneration, which has set the heart right, by giving it a new spiritual inclination, for as long as the heart is not *set right* by grace as to its habitual frame, no means can *keep it right* with God. Self is the poise of the unrenewed heart, which biases and moves it in all its designs and actions; and as long as it is so, it is impossible that any external means should keep it with God.

Man, originally, was of one constant, uniform frame of spirit, held one straight and even course; not one thought or faculty was disordered: his mind had a perfect knowledge of the requirements of God, his will a perfect compliance therewith; all his appetites and powers stood in a most obedient subordination.

Man, by the apostacy, is become a most disordered and rebellious creature, opposing his Maker, as the *First Cause*, by self-dependence; as the *Chief Good*, by self-love; as the *Highest Lord*, by self-will; and as the *Last End*, by self-seeking.

Thus he is quite disordered, and all his actions are irregular. But by regeneration the disordered soul is set right; this great change being, as the Scripture expresses it, the renovation of the soul after the image of God, in which *self-dependence* is removed by faith; *self-love*, by subjection and obedience to the will of God; and *self-seeking* by self-denial. The darkened understanding is illuminated, the refractory will sweetly subdued, the rebellious appetite gradually conquered. Thus the soul which sin had universally depraved, is by grace restored. This being pre-supposed, it will not be difficult to apprehend what it is to keep the heart, which is nothing but *the constant care and diligence of such a renewed man to preserve his soul in that holy frame to which grace has raised it.* For though grace has, in a great measure, rectified the soul, and given it an habitual heavenly temper; yet sin often actually discomposes it again; so that even a gracious heart is like a musical instrument, which though it be exactly tuned, a small matter brings it out of tune again; yea, hand it aside but a little, and it will need setting again before another lesson can be played upon it. If gracious hearts are in a desirable frame in one duty, yet how dull, dead, and disordered when they come to another! Therefore every duty needs a particular preparation of the heart. 'If thou prepare thine heart and stretch out thine hands toward him...' To keep the heart then, is carefully to preserve it from sin, which disorders it; and maintain that spiritual frame which fits it for a life of communion with God.

This includes in it six particulars:

1. Frequent observation of the frame of the heart. Carnal and formal persons take no heed to this; they cannot be brought to confer with their own hearts: there are some people who have lived forty or fifty years in the world,

and have had scarcely one hour's discourse with their own hearts. It is a hard thing to bring a man and himself together on such business; but saints know those soliloquies to be very salutary. The heathen could say, 'the soul is made wise by sitting still in quietness.' Though bankrupts care not to look into their accounts, yet upright hearts will know whether they go backward or forward. 'I commune with mine own heart,' says David. The heart can never be kept until its case be examined and understood.

2. It includes deep humiliation for heart evils and disorders; thus Hezekiah humbled himself for the pride of his heart. Thus the people were ordered to spread forth their hands to God in prayer, realizing the plague of their own hearts. Upon this account many an upright heart has been laid low before God; '*O what an heart have I.*' Saints have in their confession pointed at the heart, the pained place: '*Lord, here is the wound.*' It is with the heart well kept, as it is with the eye; if a small dust get into the eye it will never cease twinkling and watering till it has wept it out: so the upright heart cannot be at rest till it has wept out its troubles and poured out its complaints before the Lord.

3. It includes earnest supplication and instant prayer for purifying and rectifying grace when sin has defiled and disordered the heart. 'Cleanse thou me from secret faults.' 'Unite my heart to fear thy name.' Saints have always many such petitions before the throne of God's grace; this is the thing which is most pleaded by them with God. When they are praying for outward mercies, perhaps their spirits may be more remiss; but when it comes to the heart's case, they extend their spirits to the utmost, fill their mouths with arguments, weep and make supplication: 'O for a better

heart! Oh for a heart to love God more; to hate sin more; to walk more evenly with God. Lord! deny not to me such a heart, whatever thou deny me: give me a heart to fear thee, to love and delight in thee, if I beg my bread in desolate places.' It is observed of an eminent saint, that when he was confessing sin, he would never give over confessing until he had felt some brokenness of heart for that sin; and when praying for any spiritual mercy, would never give over that suit till he had obtained some relish of that mercy.

4. It includes the imposing of strong engagements upon ourselves to walk more carefully with God, and avoid the occasions whereby the heart may be induced to sin. Well advised and deliberate vows are, in some cases, very useful to guard the heart against some special sin. 'I have made a covenant with mine eyes,' says Job. By this means holy men have overawed their souls, and preserved themselves from defilement.

5. It includes a constant and holy jealousy over our own hearts. Quick sighted self-jealousy is an excellent preservative from sin. He that will keep his heart, must have the eyes of the soul awake and open upon all the disorderly and tumultuous stirrings of his affections; if the affections break loose, and the passions be stirred, the soul must discover it, and suppress them before they get to a height. 'O my soul, dost thou well in this? My tumultuous thoughts and passions, where is your commission?' Happy is the man that thus feareth always. By this fear of the Lord it is that men depart from evil, shake off sloth and preserve themselves from iniquity. He that will keep his heart must eat and drink with fear, rejoice with fear, and pass the whole time of his sojourning here in fear. All this is little enough to keep the heart from sin.

6. It includes the realizing of God's presence with us, and setting the Lord always before us. This the people have found a powerful means of keeping their hearts upright, and awing them from sin. When the eye of our faith is fixed upon the eye of God's omniscience, we dare not let out our thoughts and affections to vanity. Holy Job durst not suffer his heart to yield to an impure, vain thought, and what was it that moved him to so great circumspection? He tells us, 'Doth not He see my ways, and count all my steps?'

In such particulars as these do gracious souls express the care they have of their hearts. They are careful to prevent the breaking loose of the corruptions in time of temptation; careful to preserve the sweetness and comfort they have got from God in any duty. This is the work, and of all works in religion it is the most difficult, constant, and important work.

(i) It is the hardest work. Heart-work is hard work indeed. To shuffle over religious duties with a loose and heedless spirit, will cost no great pains; but to set thyself before the Lord, and tie up thy loose and vain thoughts to a constant and serious attendance upon him; this will cost thee something. To attain a facility and dexterity of language in prayer, and put thy meaning into apt and decent expressions, is easy; but to get thy heart broken for sin, while thou art confessing it; melted with free grace while thou art blessing God for it; to be really ashamed and humbled through the apprehensions of God's infinite holiness, and to keep thy heart in this frame, not only in, but after duty, will surely cost thee some groans and pains of soul. To repress the outward acts of sin, and compose the external part of thy life in a laudable manner, is no great matter; even carnal persons, by the force of common principles, can do this: but to kill the root of corruption within, to set and keep up an holy government over thy thoughts, to have all things lie straight and orderly in the heart, this is not easy.

(ii) It is a constant work. The keeping of the heart is a work that is never done till life is ended. There is no time or condition in the life of a Christian which will suffer an intermission of this work. It is in keeping watch over our hearts, as it was in keeping up Moses' hands while Israel and Amalek were fighting. No sooner do the hands of Moses grow heavy and sink down, than Amalek prevails. Intermitting the watch over their own hearts for but a few minutes, cost David and Peter many a sad day and night.

(iii) It is the most important business of a Christian's life. Without this we are but formalists in religion: all our professions, gifts and duties signify nothing. 'My son, give me thine heart,' is God's request. God is pleased to call that a gift which is indeed a debt; he will put this honour upon the creature, to receive it from him in the way of a gift; but if this be not given him, he regards not whatever else you bring to him. There is only so much of worth in what we do, as there is of heart in it. Concerning the heart, God seems to say, as Joseph of Benjamin, 'If you bring not Benjamin with you, you shall not see my face.' Among the Heathen, when the beast was cut up for sacrifice, the first thing the priest looked upon was the heart; and if that was unsound and worthless the sacrifice was rejected. God rejects all duties (how glorious soever in other respects) which are offered him without the heart. He that performs duty without the heart, that is, heedlessly, is no more accepted with God than he that performs it with a double heart, that is, hypocritically.

Thus I have briefly considered what the keeping of the heart supposes and imports. I proceed:

2

Assign Some Reasons Why Christians Must Make This the Great Business of Their Lives

The importance and necessity of making this our great business will manifestly appear from several considerations:

1. The glory of God is much concerned. Heart-evils are very provoking evils to the Lord. The Schools correctly observe, that outward sins are 'sins of great infamy'; but that the heart sins are 'sins of deeper guilt'. How severely has the great God declared his wrath from heaven against heart-wickedness! The crime for which the old world stands indicted is heart-wickedness! 'God saw that every imagination of their hearts was only evil, and that continually'; for which he sent the most dreadful judgments that were ever inflicted since time began. We find not their murders, adulteries, blasphemies, (though they were defiled with these) particularly alleged against them; but the evils of their hearts. That by which God was so provoked as to give up his peculiar inheritance into the enemy's hand, was the evil of their hearts. 'O Jerusalem, wash thine heart from wickedness, that thou mayest be saved; how long shall thy vain thoughts lodge within thee?'

Of the wickedness and vanity of their thoughts God took particular notice; and because of this the Chaldeans must come upon them, 'as a lion from his thicket, and tear them to pieces'. For the sin of thoughts it was that God threw down the fallen angels from heaven, and still keeps them in 'everlasting chains' to the judgment of the great day: by which expression is not obscurely intimated some extraordinary judgment to which they are reserved; as prisoners that have most irons laid upon them may be supposed to be the greatest malefactors. And what was their sin? Spiritual wickedness. Merely heart-evils are so provoking to God, that for them he rejects with indignation all the duties that some men perform. 'He that killeth an ox is as if he slew a man; he that sacrifices a lamb, as if he cut off a dog's neck; he that offereth an oblation, as if he offered swine's blood; he that burneth incense, as if he blessed an idol.' In what words could the abhorrence of a creature's actions be more fully expressed by the holy God? Murder and idolatry are not more vile in his account, than their sacrifices, though *materially* such as himself appointed. And what made their sacrifices so vile? The following words inform us: 'Their soul delighteth in their abominations.'

Such is the vileness of mere heart-sins, that the Scriptures sometimes intimate the difficulty of pardon for them. The heart of Simon Magus was not right, he had base thoughts of God, and of the things of God: the apostle bade him 'repent and pray, if perhaps the thoughts of his heart might be forgiven him'. Oh then, never slight heart evils! for by these God is highly wronged and provoked. For this reason let every Christian keep his heart with all diligence.

2. The sincerity of our profession much depends upon the care we exercise in keeping our hearts. Most certainly, that man who is careless of the frame of his heart, is but

a hypocrite in his profession, however eminent he be in the externals of religion. We have a striking instance of this in the history of Jehu. 'But Jehu took no heed to walk in the ways of the Lord God of Israel with his heart.' The context gives an account of the great service performed by Jehu against the house of Ahab and Baal, and also of the great temporal reward given him by God for that service, even that his children, to the fourth generation, should sit upon the throne of Israel. Yet in these words Jehu is censured as a hypocrite: though God approved and rewarded the work, yet he abhorred and rejected the person that did it, as hypocritical. Wherein lay the hypocrisy of Jehu? In this; he took no heed to walk in the ways of the Lord with his heart; that is, he did all insincerely and for selfish ends: and though the work he did was *materially* good, yet he, not purging his heart from those unworthy selfish designs in doing it, was a hypocrite. And though Simon Magus appeared such a person that the apostle could not regularly reject him, yet his hypocrisy was quickly discovered. Though he professed piety and associated himself with the saints, he was a stranger to the mortification of heart-sins. 'Thy heart is not right with God.' It is true, there is great difference between Christians themselves in their diligence and dexterity about heart work; some are more conversant with, and more successful in it than others: but he that takes no heed to his heart, that is not *careful* to order it aright before God, is but a hypocrite.

'And they come unto thee as the people cometh, and they sit before thee as my people, and they hear thy words, but they will not do them: for with their mouth they show much love, but their heart goeth after their covetousness.'

Here was a company of formal hypocrites, as is evident from that expression, *as my people;* like them, but not of them. And what made them so? Their outside was fair; here were reverent postures, high professions, much seeming delight in ordinances; 'thou art to them as a lovely song': yea, but for all that they kept not their hearts with God in those duties; their hearts were commanded by their lusts, they went after their covetousness. Had they kept their hearts with God, all had been well: but not regarding which way their hearts went in duty, there lay the essence of their hypocrisy.

If any upright soul should hence infer, 'I am a hypocrite too, for many times my heart departs from God in duty; do what I can, yet I cannot hold it close with God;' I answer, the very objection carries in it its own solution. Thou sayest, 'Do what I can, yet I cannot keep my heart with God.' Soul, if thou doest what thou canst, thou hast the blessing of an upright, though God sees good to exercise thee under the affliction of a discomposed heart.

There still remains some wildness in the thoughts and fancies of the best to humble them; but if you find a care before to prevent them, and opposition against them when they come, and grief and sorrow afterward, you find enough to clear you from the charge of reigning hypocrisy. This precaution is seen partly in laying up the word in thy heart to prevent them. 'Thy word have I hid in mine heart, that I might not sin against thee.' Partly in your endeavours to engage your heart to God; and partly in begging preventing grace from God in your commencement of duty. It is a good sign to exercise such precaution. And it is an evidence of uprightness, to oppose these sins in their first rise. 'I hate vain thoughts.' 'The spirit lusteth against the flesh.' Thy grief also discovers the uprightness of thy heart. If with Hezekiah thou art humbled for the evils of thy heart, thou hast no reason, from those disorders, to question the integrity of it; but to suffer sin to lodge quietly in the heart, to let thy heart habitually and without control wander from God, is a sad, a dangerous symptom indeed.

3. The beauty of our conversation arises from the heavenly frame of our spirits. There is a spiritual lustre and beauty in the conversation of saints. 'The righteous is more excellent than his neighbour;' saints shine as the lights of the world; but whatever lustre and beauty is in their lives, comes from the excellency of their spirits; as the candle within puts lustre upon the lantern in which it shines. It is impossible that a disordered and neglected heart should ever produce well-ordered conversation; and since (as the text observes) the issues or streams of life flow out of the heart as their fountain, it must follow, that such as the heart is, the life will be. Hence 1 Peter 2:11-12: 'Abstain from fleshly lusts ... having your conversation honest,' or beautiful, as the Greek word imports. So Isaiah 55:7: 'Let the wicked forsake his way, and the unrighteous man his thoughts.' *His way*, denotes the course of his life; *his thoughts*, the frame of his heart: and therefore since the course of his life flows from his thoughts, or the frame of his heart, both nor neither will be forsaken. The heart is the source of all actions; these actions are virtually and radically contained in our thoughts; these thoughts being once made up into affections, are quickly made out into suitable actions. If the heart be wicked, then, as Christ says, 'Out of the heart proceed evil thoughts, murders' etc. Mark the order: first, wanton or revengeful thoughts then unclean, or murderous practices. And if the heart be holy, then it is as with David:

'My heart is inditing a good matter – I speak of the things which I have made; my tongue is as the pen of a ready writer.' Here is a life richly beautified with good works, some ready made – *I will speak of the things which I have made;* others making – *my heart is inditing;* both proceed from the heavenly frame of his heart. Put the heart in frame and the life will quickly discover that it is so.

It is not very difficult to discern, by the performances and converse of Christians, what frames their spirits are in. Take a Christian in a good frame, and how serious, heavenly and profitable will his conversation and religious exercises be! What a lovely companion is he during the continuance of it! It would do any one's heart good to be with him at such a time. 'The mouth of the righteous speaketh wisdom, and his tongue talketh of judgment; the law of his God is in his heart.' When the heart is up with God, and full of God, how dexterously will he insinuate spiritual discourse, improving every occasion and advantage to some heavenly purpose! Few words then run to waste. And what can be the reason that the discourses and duties of many Christians are become so frothy and unprofitable, their communion both with God and with one another becomes as a dry stalk, but this, their hearts are neglected? Surely this must be the reason of it and it is an evil greatly to be bewailed.

Thus the attracting beauty that was wont to shine, from the conversation of the saints, upon the faces and consciences of the world (which, if it did not allure and bring them in love with the ways of God, at least left a testimony in their consciences of the excellency of those men and of their ways), is in a great measure lost, to the unspeakable detriment of religion.

Time was, when Christians conducted in such a manner that the world stood gazing at them. Their life and language were of a different strain from those of others; their tongues discovered them to be *Galileans* wherever they came. But now, since vain speculations and fruitless controversies have so much obtained, and heart-work, practical godliness is so much neglected among professors, the case is sadly altered: their discourse is become like other men's; if they come among you now, they may 'hear every man speak in his own language'. And I have little hope of seeing this evil redressed, and the credit of religion repaired, till Christians do their first works, till they apply again to heart-work: when the salt of heavenly-mindedness is cast into the spring, the streams will run more clear and more sweet.

4. The comfort of our souls much depends upon the keeping of our hearts; for he that is negligent in attending to his own heart, is, ordinarily, a great stranger to assurance, and the comforts following from it. Indeed if the Antinomian doctrine were true, which teaches you to reject all marks and signs for the trial of your condition, telling you that it is the Spirit that immediately assures you, by witnessing your adoption directly, *without them;* then you might be careless of your hearts, yea, strangers to them, and yet no strangers to comfort: but since both Scripture and experience confute this, I hope you will never look for comfort in this unscriptural way.

I deny not that it is the work and office of the Spirit to assure you; yet I confidently affirm, that if ever you attain assurance in the ordinary way wherein God dispenses it, you must take pains with your own hearts. You may *expect* your comforts upon *easier* terms, but I am mistaken if ever you *enjoy* them upon *any other: give all diligence; prove yourselves;* this is the scriptural method.

A distinguished writer, in his treatise on the covenant, tells us that he knew a Christian who, in the infancy of his Christianity, so vehemently panted after the infallible assurance of God's love, that for a long time together he earnestly desired some voice from heaven; yea, sometimes walking in the solitary fields, earnestly desired some miraculous voice from the trees and stones there: this, after many desires and longings, was denied; but in time a better was afforded in the ordinary way of searching the word and his own heart.

An instance of the like nature another learned person gives us of one that was driven by temptation upon the very borders of despair; at last, being sweetly settled and assured, one asked him how he attained it. He answered, 'Not by any extraordinary revelation, but by subjecting my understanding to the Scriptures, and comparing my heart with them.'

The Spirit, indeed, assures by witnessing our adoption; and he witnesses in two ways. One way is, objectively, that is, by producing those graces in our souls which are the conditions of the promise; and so the Spirit, and his graces in us, are all one: the Spirit of God dwelling in us, is a mark of our adoption. Now the Spirit can be discerned, not in his essence, but in his operations; and to discern these, is to discern the Spirit; and how these can be discerned without serious searching and diligent watching of the heart I cannot imagine. The other way of the Spirit's witnessing is effectively, that is, by irradiating the soul with a grace discovering light, shining upon his own work; and this, in order of nature, follows the former work: he first infuses the grace, and then opens the eye of the soul to see it. Now, since the heart is the subject of that infused grace, even this way of the Spirit's witnessing includes the necessity of carefully keeping our own hearts. For,

(i) A neglected heart is so confused and dark, that the little grace which is in it is not ordinarily discernible: the most accurate and laborious Christians sometimes find it difficult to discover the pure and genuine workings of the Spirit in their hearts. How then shall the Christian who is comparatively negligent about heart-work, be ever able to discover grace? Sincerity! which is the thing sought, lies in the heart like a small piece of gold in the bottom of a river; he that would find it must stay till the water is clear, and then he will see it sparkling at the bottom. That the heart may be clear and settled, how much pains and watching, care and diligence, are requisite!

(ii) God does not usually indulge negligent souls with the comforts of assurance; he will not so much as seem to patronize sloth and carelessness. He will give assurance, but it shall be in his own way; his command hath united our care and comfort together. Those are mistaken who think that assurance may be obtained without labour. Ah! how many solitary hours have the people of God spent in heart-examination! how many times have they looked into the word, and then into their hearts! Sometimes they thought they discovered sincerity, and were even ready to draw forth the triumphant conclusion of assurance; then comes a doubt they cannot resolve, and destroys it all: many hopes and fears, doubtings and reasonings, they have had in their own breasts before they arrived at a comfortable settlement. But suppose it possible for a careless Christian to attain assurance, yet it is impossible for him long to retain it; for it is a thousand to one if those whose hearts are filled with the joys of assurance, long retain those joys, unless extraordinary care be used. A little pride, vanity, or carelessness will dash to pieces all that for which they have been a long time labouring in many a weary duty. Since then the joy of our life, the comfort of our souls, rises and falls with our diligence in this work, keep your heart with all diligence.

5. The improvement of our graces depends on the keeping of our hearts. I never knew grace to thrive in a careless soul. The habits and roots of grace are planted in the heart; and the deeper they are rooted there, the more flourishing grace is. In Ephesians 3:17, we read of being 'rooted' in grace; grace in the heart is the root of every gracious work in the mouth, and of every holy work in the hand. It is true, Christ is the root of a Christian, but Christ is the originating root, and grace a root originated, planted, and influenced by Christ; accordingly, as this thrives under divine influences, the acts of grace are more or less fruitful or vigorous. Now, in a heart not kept with care and diligence, these fructifying influences are stopped and cut off – multitudes of vanities break in upon it, and devour its strength; the heart is, as it were, the inclosure, in which multitudes of thoughts are fed every day; a gracious heart, diligently kept, feeds many precious thoughts of God in a day. 'How precious are thy thoughts unto me, O God! how great is the sum of them! If I should count them, they are more in number than the sand: when I awake, I am still with thee.' And as the gracious heart nourishes them, so they refresh and feast the heart. 'My soul is filled as with marrow and fatness while I think upon thee ...'

But in the disregarded heart, multitudes of vain and foolish thoughts are perpetually working, and drive out those spiritual thoughts of God by which the soul should be refreshed. Besides, the careless heart profits nothing by any duty or ordinance it performs or attends upon, and yet these are the conduits of heaven, whence grace is watered and made fruitful. A man may go with a heedless spirit from ordinance to ordinance, abide all his days under the choicest teaching, and yet never be improved by them; for heart-neglect is a leak in the bottom – no heavenly influences, however rich, abide in that soul. When the seed falls upon the heart that lies open and common, like the highway, free for all passengers, the fowls come and devour it. Alas! it is not enough to hear, unless we take heed how we hear; a man may pray, and never be the better, unless he watch unto prayer. In a word, all means are blessed to the improvement of grace, according to the care and strictness we use in keeping our hearts in them.

6. The stability of our souls in the hour of temptation depends upon the care we exercise in keeping our hearts. The careless heart is an easy prey to Satan in the hour of temptation; his principal batteries are raised against the heart; if he wins that, he wins all, for it commands the whole man: and alas! how easy a conquest is a neglected heart! It is not more difficult to surprise such a heart, than for an enemy to enter that city whose gates are opened and unguarded. It is the watchful heart that discovers and suppresses the temptation before it comes to its strength.

Divines observe this to be the method in which temptations are ripened and brought to their full strength. There is the irritation of the object, or that power it has to provoke our corrupt nature; which is either done by the real presence of the object, or by speculation when the object (though absent) is held out by the imagination before the soul. Then follows the motion of the appetite, which is provoked by the fancy representing it as a sensual good. Then there is a consultation in the mind about the best means of accomplishing it. Next follows the election, or choice of the will. And lastly, the desire, or full engagement of the will to it.

All this may be done in a few minutes, for the debates of the soul are quick and soon ended: when it comes thus far, the heart is won, Satan hath entered victoriously and displayed his colours upon the walls of that royal fort; but, had the heart been well-guarded at first, it had never come to this – the temptation had been stopped in the first or second act. And indeed there it is stopped easily; for it is in the motion of a soul tempted to sin, as in the motion of a stone falling from the brow of a hill – it is easily stopped at first, but when once it is set in motion 'it acquires strength by descending'. Therefore it is the greatest wisdom to observe the first motions of the heart, to check and stop sin there. The motions of sin are weakest at first; a little care and watchfulness may prevent much mischief now; the careless heart not heeding this, is brought within the power of temptation, as the Syrians were brought blindfold into the midst of Samaria, before they knew where they were.

I hope that these considerations satisfy my readers that it is important to keep the heart with all diligence. I proceed:

3

Special Seasons in the Life of a Christian which Require our Utmost Diligence in Keeping the Heart

Though (as was observed before) the duty is always binding, and there is no time or condition of life in which we may be excused from this work; yet there are some signal seasons, critical hours, requiring more than common vigilance over the heart.

The *first season* is the time of prosperity, when Providence smiles upon us. Now, Christian, keep thy heart with all diligence; for it will be very apt to grow secure, proud and earthly. 'To see a man humble in prosperity,' says Bernard, 'is one of the greatest rarities in the world.' Even a good Hezekiah could not hide a vain-glorious temper in his temptation; hence that caution to Israel: 'And it shall be, when the Lord thy God shall have brought thee into the land which he sware to thy fathers, to Abraham, to Isaac, and to Jacob, to give thee great and goodly cities which thou buildedst not... then beware lest thou forget the Lord.' So indeed it happened: for 'Jeshurun waxed fat and kicked'. How then may a Christian keep his heart from pride and carnal security under the smiles of Providence and the confluence of creature-comforts?

There are several helps to secure the heart from the dangerous snares of prosperity.

1. Consider the dangerous ensnaring temptations attending a pleasant and prosperous condition. Few, very few of those that live in the pleasures of this world, escape everlasting perdition. 'It is easier,' says Christ, 'for a camel to pass through the eye of a needle, than for a rich man to enter into the kingdom of heaven.' 'Not many mighty, not many noble are called.'

We have great reason to tremble, when the Scripture tells us in general that few shall be saved; much more when it tells us, that of that rank of which we are, but few shall be saved. When Joshua called all the tribes of Israel to cast lots for the discovery of Achan, doubtless Achan feared; when the tribe of Judah was taken, his fear increased; but when the family of the Zarhites was taken, it was time to tremble. So when the Scriptures come so near as to tell us that of such a class of men very few shall escape, it is time to be alarmed. 'I should wonder,' says Chrysostom, 'if any of the *rulers* be saved.' Oh how many have been wheeled to hell in the chariots of earthly pleasures, while others have been whipped to heaven by the rod of affliction! How few, like the daughter of Tyre, come to Christ with a gift! How few among the rich entreat his favour!

2. It may keep one more humble and watchful in prosperity, to consider that among Christians many have been much the worse for it. How good had it been for some of them, if they had never known prosperity! When they were in a low condition, how humble, spiritual and heavenly they

were! But when advanced, what an apparent alteration has been upon their spirits! It was so with Israel; when they were in a low condition in the wilderness, then Israel was 'holiness to the Lord'; but when they came into Canaan and were richly fed, their language was, 'We are lords, we will come no more unto thee.' Outward gains are ordinarily attended with inward losses; as in a low condition their civil employments were wont to have a savour of their religious duties, so in an exalted condition their duties commonly have a savour of the world. He, indeed, is rich in grace whose graces are not hindered by his riches. There are but few Jehoshaphats in the world, of whom it is said, 'He had silver and gold in abundance, and his heart was lifted up in the way of God's commands.' Will not this keep thy heart humble in prosperity, to think how dearly many godly men have paid for their riches; that through them they have lost that which all the world cannot purchase?

3. Keep down thy vain heart by this consideration; God values no man the more for these things. God values no man by outward excellencies, but by inward graces; they are the internal ornaments of the Spirit, which are of great price in God's sight. God despises all worldly glory, and accepts no man's person; 'but in every nation, he that feareth God and worketh righteousness is accepted of him'. Indeed, if the judgment of God went by the same rule that man's does, we might value ourselves by these things, and stand upon them: but so much every man is, as he is in the judgment of God. Does thy heart yet swell, and will neither of the former considerations keep it humble?

4. Consider how bitterly many dying persons have bewailed their folly in setting their hearts upon these things, and have

wished that they had never known them. How dreadful was the situation of Pius Quintus, who died crying out despairingly, 'When I was in a low condition I had some hopes of salvation; when I was advanced to be a cardinal, I greatly doubted; but since I came to the popedom I have no hope at all.' An author also tells us a real, but sad story of a rich oppressor, which had scraped up a great estate for his only son: when he came to die he called his son to him, and said, 'Son, do you indeed love me?' The son answered that 'Nature, besides his paternal indulgence, obliged him to that.' 'Then,' said the father, 'express it by this: hold thy finger in the candle as long as I am saying a prayer.' The son attempted, but could not endure it. Upon that the father broke out into these expressions: 'Thou canst not suffer the burning of thy finger for me; but to get this wealth I have hazarded my soul for thee, and must burn, body and soul, in hell, for thy sake; thy pains would have been but for a moment, but mine will be unquenchable fire.'

5. The heart may be kept humble by considering of what a clogging nature earthly things are to a soul heartily engaged in the way to heaven. They shut out much of heaven from us at present, though they may not shut us out of heaven at last. If thou consider thyself as a stranger in this world, travelling for heaven, thou hast then as much reason to be delighted with these things as a weary horse has to be pleased with a heavy burden. There was a serious truth in the atheistical scoff of Julian: when taking away the Christians' estates, he told them 'it was to make them more fit for the kingdom of heaven.'

6. Is thy spirit still vain and lofty? Then urge upon it the consideration of that awful day of reckoning, wherein,

according to our receipt of mercies, shall be our account for them. Methinks this should awe and humble the vainest heart that ever was in the breast of a saint. Know for a certainty that the Lord records all the mercies that ever he gave thee, from the beginning to the end of thy life. 'Remember, Oh my people, from Shittim unto Gilgal...' Yes, they are exactly numbered and recorded in order to an account; and thy account will be suitable: 'To whomsoever much is given, of him shall much be required.' You are but a steward, and your Lord will come and take an account of you; and what a great account have you to make, who have much of this world in your hands! What swift witnesses will your mercies be against you, if this be the best fruit of them!

7. It is a very humbling reflection, that the mercies of God should work otherwise upon my spirit than they used to do upon the spirits of others to whom they come as sanctified mercies from the love of God. Ah, Lord! What a sad consideration is this! Enough to lay me in the dust, when I consider:

(i) That their mercies have greatly humbled them; the higher God has raised them, the lower they have laid themselves before him. Thus did Jacob when God had given him much substance. 'And Jacob said, I am not worthy of the least of all thy mercies, and all the truth which thou hast showed thy servant; for with my staff I passed over this Jordan, and am now become two bands.' Thus also it was with holy David; when God had confirmed the promise to him, to build him a house, and not reject him as he did Saul, he goes in before the Lord and says, 'Who am I, and what is my father's house, that thou hast brought me hitherto?' So indeed God required. When Israel brought to him the first fruits of Canaan, they were to say, 'A Syrian ready to perish was my father...' Do others raise God the higher for his raising them? And the more God raises me, the more shall I abuse him and exalt myself? Oh how wicked is such conduct as this!

(ii) Others have freely ascribed the glory of all their enjoyments to God, and magnified not themselves, but him, for their mercies. Thus says David, 'Let thy name be magnified and the house of thy servant be established.' He does not fly upon the mercy and suck out its sweetness, looking no further than his own comfort: no, he cares for no mercy except God be magnified in it. So when God had delivered him from all his enemies, he says, 'The Lord is my strength and my rock, he is become my salvation.' Saints of old did not put the crown upon their own heads as I do by my vanity.

(iii) The mercies of God have been melting mercies unto others, melting their souls in love to the God of their mercies. When Hannah received the mercy of a son, she said, 'My soul rejoiceth in the Lord'; not in the mercy, but in the God of mercy. So also Mary: 'My soul doth magnify the Lord; my spirit rejoiceth in God my Saviour.' The word signifies to make more room for God; their hearts were not contracted, but the more enlarged to God.

(iv) The mercies of God have been great restraints to keep others from sin. 'Seeing thou, our God, hast given us such a deliverance as this, should we again break thy commandments?' Ingenuous souls have felt the force of the obligations of love and mercy upon them.

(v) The mercies of God to others have been as oil to the wheels of their obedience, and made them more fit for service. Now if mercies work contrarily upon my heart, what cause have I to be afraid that they come not to me in love! It is enough to damp the spirits of any saint, to see what sweet effects mercies have had upon others, and what bitter effects upon him.

The *second season* in the life of a Christian, requiring more than common diligence to keep his heart, is the time of *adversity*. When Providence frowns upon you, and blasts your outward comforts, then look to your heart; keep it with all diligence from repining against God, or fainting under his hand; for troubles, though sanctified, are troubles still. Jonah was a good man, and yet how fretful was his heart under affliction! Job was the mirror of patience, yet how was his heart discomposed by trouble! You will find it hard to get a composed spirit under great afflictions. Oh the hurries and tumults which they occasion even in the best hearts! Let me show you, then, how a Christian under great afflictions may keep his heart from repining or desponding, under the hand of God.

I will here offer several helps to keep the heart in this condition.

1. By these cross providences God is faithfully pursuing the great design of electing love upon the souls of his people, and orders all these afflictions as means sanctified to that end. Afflictions come not by casualty, but by counsel. By this counsel of God they are ordained as means of much spiritual good to saints. 'By this shall the iniquity of Jacob be purged...' 'But he for our profit...' 'All things work together for good...' They are God's workmen upon our hearts, to pull down the pride and carnal security of them; and being so, their nature is changed; they are turned into blessings and benefits. 'It is good for me that I have been afflicted,' says David. Surely then thou hast no reason to

quarrel with God, but rather to wonder that he should concern himself so much in thy good as to use any means for accomplishing it. Paul could bless God if by any means he might attain the resurrection of the dead. 'My brethren,' says James, 'count it all joy when you fall into divers temptations.' 'My Father is about a design of love upon my soul, and do I well to be angry with him? All that he does is in pursuance of, and in reference to some eternal, glorious ends upon my soul. It is my ignorance of God's design that makes me quarrel with him.' He says to thee in this case, as he did to Peter, 'What I do, thou knowest not now, but thou shalt know hereafter.'

2. Though God has reserved to himself a liberty of afflicting his people, yet he has tied up his own hands by promise never to take away his loving kindness from them. Can I contemplate this scripture with a repining, discontented spirit: 'I will be his Father, and he shall be my son: if he commit iniquity, I will chasten him with the rod of man, and with the stripes of the children of men: nevertheless my mercy shall not depart away from him'? O my heart, my haughty heart! Dost thou well to be discontent, when God has given thee the whole tree, with all the clusters of comfort growing on it, because he suffers the wind to blow down a few leaves? Christians have two kinds of goods; the goods of the throne and the goods of the footstool; immoveables and moveables. If God has secured those, never let my heart be troubled at the loss of these: indeed, if he had cut off his love, or discovenanted my soul, I had reason to be cast down; but this he hath not done, nor can he do it.

3. It is of great efficacy to keep the heart from sinking under afflictions, to call to mind that thine own Father has the

ordering of them. Not a creature moves hand or tongue against thee but by his permission. Suppose the cup be bitter, yet it is the cup which thy Father hath given thee; and canst thou suspect poison to be in it? Foolish man, put home the case to thine own heart; canst thou give thy child that which would ruin him? No! thou wouldst as soon hurt thyself as him. 'If thou then, being evil, knowest how to give good gifts to thy children', how much more does God! The very consideration of his nature as a God of love, pity, and tender mercies; or of his relation to thee as a father, husband, friend, may be security enough, if he had not spoken a word to quiet thee in this case; and yet you have his word too, by the prophet Jeremiah: 'I will do you no hurt.' You lie too near his heart for him to hurt you; nothing grieves him more than your groundless and unworthy suspicions of his designs. Would it not grieve a faithful, tender-hearted physician, when he had studied the case of his patient, and prepared the most excellent medicines to save his life, to hear him cry out, 'Oh he has undone me! he has poisoned me!' because it pains him in the operation? Oh when will you be ingenuous?

4. God respects you as much in a low as in a high condition; and therefore it need not so much trouble you to be made low; nay, he manifests more of his love, grace and tenderness in the time of affliction than in the time of prosperity. As God did not at first choose you because you were high, he will not now forsake you because you are low. Men may look shy upon you, and alter their respects as your condition is altered; when Providence has blasted your estate, your summer-friends may grow strange, fearing you may be troublesome to them; but will God do so? No, no: 'I will never leave thee nor forsake thee,' says he. If adversity and

poverty could bar you from access to God, it were indeed a deplorable condition: but, so far from this, you may go to him as freely as ever. 'My God will hear me,' says the church. Poor David, when stripped of all earthly comforts, could encourage himself in the Lord his God; and why cannot you? Suppose your husband or son had lost all at sea, and should come to you in rags; could you deny the relation, or refuse to entertain him? If you would not, much less will God. Why then are you so troubled? Though your condition be changed, your Father's love is not changed.

5. What if by the loss of outward comforts God preserves your soul from the ruining power of temptation? Surely then you have little cause to sink your heart by such sad thoughts. Do not earthly enjoyments make men shrink and warp in times of trial? For the love of these many have forsaken Christ in such an hour. The young ruler 'went away sorrowful, for he had great possessions'. If this is God's design, how ungrateful to murmur against him for it! We see mariners in a storm can throw over-board the most valuable goods to preserve their lives. We know it is usual for soldiers in a besieged city to destroy the finest buildings without the walls in which the enemy may take shelter; and no one doubts that it is wisely done. Those who have mortified limbs willingly stretch them out to be cut off, and not only thank, but pay the surgeon. Must God be murmured against for casting over that which would sink you in a storm; for pulling down that which would assist your enemy in the siege of temptation; for cutting off what would endanger your everlasting life? Oh, inconsiderate, ungrateful man! Are not these things for which thou grievest, the very things that have ruined thousands of souls?

6. It would much support thy heart under adversity, to consider that God by such humbling providences may be accomplishing that for which you have long prayed and waited. And should you be troubled at that? Say, Christian, hast thou not many prayers depending before God upon such accounts as these; that he would keep thee from sin; discover to thee the emptiness of the creature; that he would mortify and kill thy lusts; that thy heart may never find rest in any enjoyment but Christ? By such humbling and impoverishing strokes God may be fulfilling thy desire.

Wouldst thou be kept from sin? *Lo, he hath hedged up thy way with thorns.* Wouldst thou see the creature's vanity? Thy affliction is a fair glass to discover it; for the vanity of the creature is never so effectually and sensibly discovered, as in our own experience. Wouldst thou have thy corruptions mortified? This is the way: to have the food and fuel removed that maintained them; for as prosperity begat and fed them, so adversity, when sanctified, is a means to kill them. Wouldst thou have thy heart rest nowhere but in the bosom of God? What better method could Providence take to accomplish thy desire than pulling from under thy head that soft pillow of creature-delights on which you rested before?

And yet you fret at this: peevish child, how dost thou try thy Father's patience! If he delay to answer thy prayers, thou art ready to say he regards thee not; if he does that which really answers the end of them, though not in the way which you expect, you murmur against him for that; as if instead of answering, he were crossing all thy hopes and aims. Is this ingenuous? Is it not enough that God is so gracious as to do what thou desirest: must thou be so impudent as to expect him to do it in the way which thou prescribest?

7. It may support thy heart, to consider that in these troubles God is performing that work in which thy soul would rejoice, if thou didst see the design of it. We are clouded with much ignorance, and are not able to discern how particular providences tend to the fulfilment of God's designs; and therefore, like Israel in the wilderness, are often murmuring, because Providence leads us about in a howling desert, where we are exposed to difficulties; though then he led them, and is now leading us, *by the right way to a city of habitations.* If you could but see how God in his secret counsel has exactly laid the whole plan of your salvation, even to the smallest means and circumstances; could you but discern the admirable harmony of divine dispensations, their mutual relations, together with the general respect they all have to the last end; had you liberty to make your own choice, you would, of all conditions in the world, choose that in which you now are. Providence is like a curious piece of tapestry made of a thousand shreds, which, single, appear useless, but put together, they represent a beautiful history to the eye. As God does all things according to the counsel of his own will, of course this is ordained as the best method to effect your salvation. *Such an one has a proud heart, so many humbling providences appoint for him; such an one has an earthly heart, so many impoverishing providences for him.* Did you but see this, I need say no more to support the most dejected heart.

8. It would much conduce to the settlement of your heart, to consider that by fretting and discontent you do yourself more injury than all your afflictions could do. Your own discontent is that which arms your troubles with a sting; you make your burden heavy by struggling under it. Did you but lie quietly under the hand of God, your condition

would be much more easy than it is. 'Impatience in the sick occasions severity in the physician.' This makes God afflict the more, as a father a stubborn child that receives not correction. Beside, it unfits the soul to pray over its troubles, or receive the sense of that good which God intends by them. Affliction is a pill, which, being wrapt up in patience and quiet submission, may be easily swallowed; but discontent chews the pill, and so embitters the soul. God throws away some comfort which he saw would hurt you, and you will throw away your peace after it; he shoots an arrow which sticks in your clothes, and was never intended to hurt, but only to drive you from sin, and you will thrust it deeper, to the piercing of your very heart, by despondency and discontent.

9. If thy heart (like that of Rachel) still refuses to be comforted, then do one thing more: compare the condition thou art now in, and with which thou art so much dissatisfied, with the condition in which others are, and in which thou deservest to be. 'Others are roaring in flames, howling under the scourge of vengeance; and among them I deserve to be. Oh my soul, is this hell? Is my condition as bad as that of the damned? What would thousands now in hell give to exchange conditions with me!' I have read (says an author) that when the Duke of Conde had voluntarily subjected himself to the inconveniences of poverty, he was one day observed and pitied by a lord of Italy, who from tenderness wished him to be more careful of his person. The good duke answered, 'Sir, be not troubled, and think not that I suffer from want; for I send a harbinger before me, who makes ready my lodgings and takes care that I be royally entertained.' The lord asked him who was his

harbinger? He answered, 'The knowledge of myself, and the consideration of what I deserve for my sins, which is eternal torment; when with this knowledge I arrive at my lodging, however unprovided I find it, methinks it is much better than I deserve. *Why doth the living man complain?*' Thus the heart may be kept from desponding or repining under adversity.

The *third season* calling for more than ordinary diligence to keep the heart is the time of *Zion's troubles*. When the church, like the ship in which Christ and his disciples were, is oppressed and ready to perish in the waves of persecution, then good souls are ready to be shipwrecked too, upon the billows of their own fears. It is true, most men need the spur rather than the reins in this case; yet some men sit down discouraged under a sense of the church's troubles. The loss of the ark cost Eli his life; and the sad posture in which Jerusalem lay made good Nehemiah's countenance change in the midst of all the pleasures and accommodations of the court. But though God allows, yea, commands the most awakened apprehensions of these calamities, and in 'such a day calls to mourning, weeping, and girding with sackcloth', and severely threatens the insensible; yet it will not please him to see you sit like pensive Elijah under the juniper tree. 'Ah, Lord God! it is enough, take away my life also.' No: a mourner in Zion you may and ought to be, but a self-tormentor you must not be; complain *to* God you may, but complain *of* God (though but by the language of your actions) you must not.

Now let us inquire how tender hearts may be relieved and supported, when they are even overwhelmed with the burdensome sense of Zion's troubles? I grant it is hard for him who preferreth Zion, to his chief joy, to keep his heart that it sink not below this due sense of its troubles; yet this ought to, and may be done, by the use of such heart-establishing directions as these:

1. Settle this great truth in your heart, that no trouble befalls Zion but by the permission of Zion's God; and he permits nothing out of which he will not ultimately bring much good to his people. Comfort may be derived from reflections on the permitting as well as on the commanding will of God. 'Let him alone, it may be God hath bidden him.' 'Thou couldst have no power against me, except it were given thee from above.' It should much calm our spirits, that it is the will of God to suffer it; and that, had he not suffered it, it could never have been as it is. This very consideration quieted Job, Eli, David, and Hezekiah. That the Lord did it was enough for them: and why should it not be so to us? If the Lord will have Zion ploughed as a field, and her goodly stones lie in the dust; if it be his pleasure that Anti-Christ shall rage yet longer and wear out the saints of the Most High; if it be his will that a day of trouble, and of treading down, and of perplexity by the Lord God of Hosts, shall be upon the valley of vision, that the wicked shall devour the man that is more righteous than he; what are we that we should contend with God?

It is fit that we should be resigned to that will whence we proceeded, and that he that made us should dispose of us as he pleases: he may do what seemeth him good without our consent. Doth poor man stand upon equal ground, that he may capitulate with his Creator; or that God should render him an account of any of his matters? That we be content, however God may dispose of us, is as reasonable as that we be obedient, whatever he may require of us. But if we pursue this argument farther, and consider that God's permissions all meet at last in the real good of his people, this will much more quiet our spirits. Do the enemies carry away the best among the people into captivity? This looks like a distressing providence; but God sends them thither for their good. Does God take the Assyrian as a staff in his hand to beat his people with?

The end of his so doing is 'that he may accomplish his whole work upon Mount Zion'. If God can bring much good out of the greatest evil of sin, much more out of temporal afflictions; and that he will, is as evident as that he can do so. For it is inconsistent with the wisdom of a common agent to permit any thing (which he might prevent if he pleased) to cross his great design; and can it be imagined that the most wise God should do so? As, then, Luther said to Melancthon, so say I to you: 'Let infinite wisdom, power and love alone'; for by these all creatures are swayed, and all actions guided, in reference to the church. It is not our work to rule the world, but to submit to him that does. The motions of Providence are all judicious, the wheels are full of eyes: it is enough that the affairs of Zion are in a good hand.

2. Ponder this heart-supporting truth: how many troubles soever are upon Zion, yet her King is in her. What! hath the Lord forsaken his churches? Has he sold them into the enemy's hands? Does he not regard what evil befalls them, that our hearts sink thus? Is it not shamefully undervaluing the great God, and too much magnifying poor impotent man, to fear and tremble at creatures while God is in the midst of us? The church's enemies are many and mighty: let that be granted, yet that argument with which Caleb and Joshua

strove to raise their own hearts, is of as much force now as it was then: 'The Lord is with us, fear them not.' A historian tells us, that when Antigonus overheard his soldiers reckoning how many their enemies were, and so discouraging one another, he suddenly stepped in among them with this question, 'And how many do you reckon me for?' Discouraged souls, how many do you reckon the Lord for? Is he not an overmatch for all his enemies? Is not *one Almighty* more than *many mighties?* 'If God be for us, who can be against us?' What think you was the reason of that great examination Gideon made? He questions, he desires a sign, and after that, another: and what was the end of all this, but that he might be sure the Lord was with him, and that he might but write this motto upon his ensign: *The sword of the Lord and of Gideon.* So if you can be well assured the Lord is with his people, you will thereby rise above all your discouragements: and that he is so, you need not require a sign from heaven; lo, you have a sign before you, even their marvellous preservation amidst all their enemies. If God be not with his people, how is it that they are not swallowed up quickly? Do their enemies want malice, power, or opportunity? No, but there is an invisible hand upon them. Let then his presence give us rest; and though the mountains be hurled into the sea, though heaven and earth mingle together, fear not; God is in the midst of Zion, she shall not be moved.

3. Consider the great advantages attending the people of God in an afflicted condition. If a low and an afflicted state in the world be really best for the church, then your dejection is not only irrational, but ungrateful. Indeed if you estimate the happiness of the church by its worldly ease, splendour and prosperity, then such times of affliction will

51

appear to be unfavourable; but if you reckon its glory to consist in its humility, faith, and heavenly-mindedness, no condition so much abounds with advantages for these as an afflicted condition. It was not persecutions and prisons, but worldliness and wantonness that poisoned the church: neither was it the earthly glory of its professors, but the blood of its martyrs that was the seed of the church. The power of godliness did never thrive better than in affliction, and was never less thriving than in times of greatest prosperity: when 'we are left a poor and an afflicted people, then we learn to trust in the name of the Lord'.

It is indeed for the saints' advantage to be weaned from love of, and delight in, ensnaring earthly vanities; to be quickened and urged forward with more haste to heaven; to have clearer discoveries of their own hearts; to be taught to pray more fervently, frequently, spiritually; to look and long for the rest to come more ardently. If these be for their advantage, experience teaches us that no condition is ordinarily blessed with such fruits as these, like an afflicted condition. Is it well then to repine and droop, because your Father consults the advantage of your soul rather than the gratification of your humours? because he will bring you to heaven by a nearer way than you are willing to go? Is this a due requital of his love, who is pleased so much to concern himself in your welfare – who does more for you than he will do for thousands in the world, upon whom he will not lay a rod, dispense an affliction to them for their good? But alas! we judge by sense, and reckon things good or evil, according to our present taste.

4. Take heed that you overlook not the many precious mercies which the people of God enjoy amidst all their trouble.

It is a pity that our tears on account of our troubles should so blind our eyes that we should not see our mercies. I will not insist upon the mercy of having your life given you for a prey; nor upon the many outward comforts which you enjoy, even above what were enjoyed by Christ and his precious servants, of whom the world was not worthy. But what say you to pardon of sin; interest in Christ; the covenant of promise; and an eternity of happiness in the presence of God, after a few days are over? Oh that a people entitled to such mercies as these should droop under any temporal affliction, or be so much concerned for the frowns of men and the loss of trifles. You have not the smiles of great men, but you have the favour of the great God; you are perhaps diminished in temporal, but you are thereby increased in spiritual and eternal goods. You cannot live so plentifully as before; but you may live as heavenly as ever. Will you grieve so much for these circumstances as to forget your substance? Shall light troubles make you forget weighty mercies? Remember the true riches of the church are laid out of the reach of all enemies. What though God do not in his outward dispensations distinguish between his own and others? Yea, what though his judgments single out the best, and spare the worst? What though an Abel be killed in love, and a Cain survive in hatred; a bloody Dionysius die in his bed, and a good Josiah fall in battle? What though the belly of the wicked be filled with hidden treasures, and the teeth of the saints with gravel-stones? Still there is much matter of praise; for *electing love* has distinguished, though *common providence* has not: and while prosperity and impunity slay the wicked, even slaying and adversity shall benefit and save the righteous.

5. Believe that how low soever the church be plunged under the waters of adversity, she shall assuredly rise again. Fear

not; for as surely as Christ arose the third day, notwithstanding the seal and watch upon him; so surely Zion shall arise out of all her troubles, and lift up her victorious head over all her enemies. There is no reason to fear the ruin of that people who thrive by their losses and multiply by being diminished. Be not too hasty to bury the church before she is dead; stay till Christ has tried his skill, before you give her up for lost. The bush may be all in a flame, but shall never be consumed; and that because of the good will of him that dwelleth in it.

6. Remember the instances of God's care and tenderness over his people in former difficulties. For above eighteen hundred years the Christian church has been in affliction, and yet it is not consumed; many a wave of persecution has gone over it, yet it is not drowned; many devices have been formed against it, hitherto none of them has prospered. This is not the first time that Hamans and Ahithophels have plotted its ruin; that a Herod has stretched out his hand to vex it; still it has been preserved from, supported under, or delivered out of all its troubles. Is it not as dear to God as ever? Is he not as able to save it now as formerly? Though we know not whence deliverance should arise, 'yet the Lord knoweth how to deliver the godly out of temptations.'

7. If you can derive no comfort from any of these considerations, try to draw some out of your very trouble. Surely this trouble of yours is a good evidence of your integrity. Union is the ground of sympathy: if you had not some rich adventure in that ship, you would not tremble as you do when it is in danger. Beside this frame of spirit may afford you this consolation, that if you are so sensible of Zion's trouble, Jesus Christ is much more sensible of and solicitous

about it than you can be, and he will have an eye of favour upon them that mourn for it.

The *fourth season*, requiring our utmost diligence to keep our hearts, is the time of *danger and public distraction*. In such times the best hearts are too apt to be surprised by slavish fear. If Syria be confederate with Ephraim, how do the hearts of the house of David shake, even as the trees of the wood which are shaken with the wind. When there are ominous signs in the heavens, or the distress of nations with perplexity, the sea and the waves roaring; then the hearts of men fail for fear, and for looking after those things which are coming on the earth. Even a Paul may sometimes complain of 'fightings within, when there are fears without'.

But, my brethren, these things ought not so to be; saints should be of a more elevated spirit; so was David when his heart was kept in a good frame: 'The Lord is my light and my salvation; whom shall I fear? the Lord is the strength of my life, of whom shall I be afraid?' Let none but the servants of sin be the slaves of fear; let them that have delighted in evil fear evil. Let not that which God has threatened as a judgment upon the wicked, ever seize upon the hearts of the righteous. 'I will send faintness into their hearts in the land of their enemies, and the sound of a shaking leaf shall chase them.' What poor spirited men are those, to fly at a shaking leaf! A leaf makes a pleasant, not a terrible noise; it makes indeed a kind of natural music: but to a guilty conscience even the whistling leaves are drums and trumpets!

'But God has not given us the spirit of fear, but of love and of a sound mind.' A *sound mind,* as it stands there in opposition to *fear*, is an unwounded conscience not weakened by guilt: and this should make a man as bold as a lion. I know it cannot be said of a saint, as God said of *leviathan*, that he is made without fear; there is a natural fear in every man, and it is as impossible to remove it wholly, as to remove the body itself. Fear is perturbation of the mind, arising from the apprehension of approaching danger; and as long as dangers can approach us, we shall find some perturbations within us. It is not my purpose to commend to you a stoical apathy, nor yet to dissuade you from such a degree of cautionary preventive fear as may fit you for trouble and be serviceable to your soul. There is a provident fear that opens our eyes to foresee danger, and quickens us to a prudent and lawful use of means to prevent it: such was Jacob's fear, and such his prudence when expecting to meet his angry brother Esau. But it is the fear of diffidence, from which I would persuade you to keep your heart; that tyrannical passion which invades the heart in times of danger, distracts, weakens and unfits it for duty, drives men upon unlawful means, and brings a snare with it.

Now let us inquire how a Christian may keep his heart from distracting and tormenting fears in times of great and threatening dangers. There are several excellent rules for keeping the heart from sinful fear when imminent dangers threaten us:

1. Look upon all creatures as in the hand of God, who manages them in all their motions, limiting, restraining and determining them at his pleasure. Get this truth well settled by faith in your heart, and it will guard you against slavish fears. The first chapter of Ezekiel contains

an admirable draught of Providence: there you see the living creatures who move the wheels (that is, the great revolutions of things here below) coming unto Christ, who sits upon the throne, to receive new instructions from him. In Revelations, sixth chapter, you read of white, black and red horses, which are but the instruments God employs in executing judgments in the world, as wars, pestilence, and death. When these horses are prancing and trampling up and down in the world, here is a consideration that may quiet our hearts; God has the reins in his hand. Wicked men are sometimes like mad horses, they would stamp the people of God under their feet, but that the bridle of Providence is in their mouths. A lion at liberty is terrible to meet, but who is afraid of a lion in the keeper's hand?

2. Remember that this God in whose hand are all creatures, is your Father, and is much more tender of you than you are, or can be, of yourself. 'He that toucheth you, toucheth the apple of mine eye.' Let me ask the most timorous woman whether there be not a great difference between the sight of a drawn sword in the hand of a bloody ruffian, and of the same sword in the hand of her own tender husband? As great a difference there is between looking upon creatures by an eye of sense, and looking on them, as in the hand of your God, by an eye of faith. Isaiah 54:5 is here very appropriate: 'Thy Maker is thine husband, the Lord of hosts is his name'; he is Lord of all the hosts of creatures. Who would be afraid to pass through an army, though all the soldiers should turn their swords and guns toward him, if the commander of that army were his friend or father? A religious young man being at sea with many other passengers in a great storm, and they being half dead with fear,

he only was observed to be very cheerful, as if he were but little concerned in that danger: one of them demanding the reason of his cheerfulness, 'Oh', said he, 'it is because the pilot of the ship is my Father!' Consider Christ first as the King and supreme Lord over the providential kingdom, and then as your head, husband and friend, and you will quickly say, 'Return unto thy rest, Oh my soul.' This truth will make you cease trembling, and cause you to sing in the midst of danger, 'The Lord is King of all the earth, sing ye praise with understanding.' That is, 'Let everyone that has understanding of this heart-reviving and establishing doctrine of the dominion of our Father over all creatures, sing praise.'

3. Urge upon your heart the express prohibitions of Christ in this case, and let your heart stand in awe of the violation of them. He hath charged you not to fear: 'When we shall hear of wars and commotions, see that ye be not terrified.' 'In nothing be terrified by your adversaries.' In Matthew 10, and within the compass of six verses, our Saviour commands us thrice, 'not to fear man'. Does the voice of a man make thee to tremble, and shall not the voice of God? If thou art of such a timorous spirit, how is it that thou fearest not to disobey the commands of Jesus Christ? Methinks the command of Christ should have as much power to calm, as the voice of a poor worm to terrify thy heart. 'I, even I, am he that comforteth you: who art thou, that thou shouldst be afraid of a man that shall die, and of the son of man that shall be made as the grass, and forgettest the Lord thy Maker?' We cannot fear creatures sinfully till we have forgotten God: did we remember what he is, and what he has said, we should not be of such feeble spirits. Bring thyself then to this reflection in times of danger: 'If

I let into my heart the slavish fear of man, I must let out the reverential awe and fear of God; and dare I cast off the fear of the Almighty for the frowns of a man? Shall I lift up proud dust above the great God? Shall I run upon a certain sin, to shun a probable danger?' O keep thy heart by this consideration!

4. Remember how much needless trouble your vain fears have brought upon you formerly: 'And hast feared continually because of the oppressor, as if he were ready to devour; and where is the fury of the oppressor?' He seemed ready to devour, yet you are not devoured. I have not brought upon you the thing that you feared; you have wasted your spirit, disordered your soul, and weakened your heads to no purpose: you might have all this while enjoyed your peace, and possessed your soul in patience. And here I cannot but observe a very deep policy of Satan in managing a design against the soul by these vain fears. I call them vain, with reference to the frustration of them by Providence; but certainly they are not in vain as the end at which Satan aims in raising them; for herein he acts as soldiers do in the siege of a garrison, who to wear out the besieged by constant watchings, and thereby unfit them to make resistance when they storm it in earnest, every night rouse them with false alarms, which though they come to nothing yet remarkably answer the ultimate design of the enemy. Oh when will you beware of Satan's devices?

5. Consider solemnly, that though the things you fear should really happen, yet there is more evil in your own fear than in the things feared: and that, not only as the least evil of sin is worse than the greatest evil of suffering; but as this sinful fear has really more trouble in it than there is in that condition of which you are so much afraid. Fear is

both a multiplying and a tormenting passion; it represents troubles as much greater than they are, and so tortures the soul much more than the suffering itself.

So it was with Israel at the Red Sea; they cried out and were afraid, till they stepped into the water, and then a passage was opened through those waters which they thought would have drowned them. Thus it is with us; we, looking through the glass of carnal fear upon the waters of trouble, the swellings of Jordan, cry out, 'Oh they are unfordable; we must perish in them!' But when we come into the midst of those floods indeed, we find the promise made good: 'God will make a way to escape.' Thus it was with a blessed martyr; when he would make a trial by putting his finger to the candle, and found himself not able to endure that, he cried out, 'What! cannot I bear the burning of a finger? How then shall I be able to bear the burning of my whole body to-morrow?' Yet when that morrow came he could go cheerfully into the flames with this scripture in his mouth: 'Fear not, for I have redeemed thee; I have called thee by thy name, thou art mine; when thou passest through the waters I will be with you; when thou walkest through the fire thou shalt not be burnt.'

6. Consult the many precious promises which are written for your support and comfort in all dangers. These are your refuges to which you may fly and be safe when the arrows of danger fly by night, and destruction wasteth at noonday. There are particular promises suited to particular cases and exigencies; there are also general promises reaching all cases and conditions. Such as these: 'All things shall work together for good...' 'Though a sinner do evil an hundred times and his days be prolonged, yet it shall be well with

them that fear the Lord...' Could you but believe the promises your heart should be established. Could you but plead
them with God as Jacob did, ('Thou saidst, I will surely do
thee good'), they would relieve you in every distress.

7. Quiet your trembling heart by recording and consult-
ing your past experiences of the care and faithfulness of
God in former distresses. These experiences are food for
your faith in a wilderness. By this David kept his heart in
time of danger, and Paul his. It was answered by a saint,
when one told him that his enemies waylaid him to take
his life: 'If God take no care of me, how is it that I have
escaped hitherto?' You may plead with God old experiences for new ones: for it is in pleading with God for new
deliverances, as it is in pleading for new pardons. Mark
how Moses pleads of that account with God. 'Pardon,
I beseech thee, the iniquity of this people, as thou hast
forgiven them from Egypt until now.' He does not say as
men do, 'Lord, this is the first fault, thou hast not been
troubled before to sign their pardon', but, 'Lord, because
thou hast pardoned them so often, I beseech thee pardon
them once again.' So in new difficulties let the saint say,
'Lord, thou hast often heard, helped and saved, in former
years; therefore now help again, for with thee there is
plenteous redemption, and thine arm is not shortened.'

8. Be well satisfied that you are in the way of your duty, and
that will beget holy courage in times of danger. 'Who will
harm you if you be a follower of that which is good?' Or
if any dare attempt to harm you 'you may boldly commit
yourself to God in well-doing'. It was this consideration
that raised Luther's spirit above all fear: 'In the cause of
God', said he, 'I ever am, and ever shall be stout: herein

I assume this title, "I yield to none".' A good cause will bear up a man's spirit. Hear the saying of a heathen, to the shame of cowardly Christians: when the emperor Vespasian had commanded Fluidus Priseus not to come to the senate, or if he did come, to speak nothing but what he would have him; the senator returned this noble answer, 'that he was a senator, it was fit he should be at the senate; and if being there, he were required to give his advice, he would freely speak that which his conscience commanded him.' The emperor threatening that then he should die; he answered, 'Did I ever tell you that I was immortal? Do what you will, and I will do what I ought. It is in your power to put me to death unjustly, and in my power to die with constancy.' Righteousness is a breastplate: let them tremble whom danger finds out of the way of duty.

9. Get your conscience sprinkled with the blood of Christ from all guilt, and that will set your heart above all fear. It is guilt upon the conscience that softens and makes cowards of our spirits: 'the righteous are bold as a lion'. It was guilt in Cain's conscience that made him cry, 'Every one that findeth me will slay me.' A guilty conscience is more terrified by imagined dangers, than a pure conscience is by real ones. A guilty sinner carries a witness against himself in his own bosom. It was guilty Herod cried out, 'John the Baptist is risen from the dead.' Such a conscience is the devil's anvil, on which he fabricates all those swords and spears with which the guilty sinner pierces himself. Guilt is to danger, what fire is to gun-powder: a man need not fear to walk among many barrels of powder, if he have no fire about him.

10. Exercise holy trust in times of great distress. Make it your business to trust God with your life and comforts, and

then your heart will be at rest about them. So did David, 'At what time I am afraid I will trust in thee'; that is, 'Lord, if at any time a storm arise, I will shelter from it under the covert of thy wings.' Go to God by acts of faith and trust, and never doubt that he will secure you. 'Thou wilt keep him in perfect peace whose mind is stayed on thee, because he trusteth in thee,' says Isaiah. God is pleased when you come to him thus: 'Father, my life, my liberty and my estate are exposed, and I cannot secure them; Oh let me leave them in thy hand. *The poor leaveth himself with thee;* and does his God fail him? No, *thou art the helper of the fatherless:* that is, thou art the helper of the destitute one, that has none to go to but God.' This is a comforting passage, 'He shall not be afraid of evil tidings, his heart is fixed, trusting in the Lord'; he does not say, his ear shall be preserved from the report of evil tidings; he may hear as sad tidings as other men, but his heart shall be kept from the terror of those tidings; *his heart is fixed.*

11. Consult the honour of religion more, and your personal safety less. Is it for the honour of religion (think you) that Christians should be as timorous as hares to start at every sound? Will not this tempt the world to think, that what ever you talk, yet your principles are no better than other men's? What mischief may the discovery of your fears before them do! It was nobly said by Nehemiah, 'Should such a man as I flee? and who, being as I am, would flee?' Were it not better you should die than that the world should be prejudiced against Christ by your example? For alas! how apt is the world (who judge more by what they see in your practices than by what they understand of your principles) to conclude from your timidity, that how much soever you

commend faith and talk of assurance, yet you dare trust to those things no more than they, when it comes to the trial. Oh let not your fears lay such a stumbling-block before the blind world.

12. He that would secure his heart from fear, must first secure the eternal interest of his soul in the hands of Jesus Christ. When this is done, you may say, 'Now, world, do thy worst!' You will not be very solicitous about a vile body, when you are once assured it shall be well to all eternity with your precious soul. 'Fear not them (says Christ) that can kill the body, and after that have no more that they can do.' The assured Christian may smile with contempt upon all his enemies, and say, 'Is this the worst that you can do?' What say you, Christian? Are you assured that your soul is safe; that within a few moments of your dissolution it shall be received by Christ into an everlasting habitation? If you be sure of that, never trouble yourself about the instrument and means of your death.

13. Learn to quench all slavish creature-fears in the reverential fear of God. This is a cure by diversion. It is an exercise of Christian wisdom to turn those passions of the soul which most predominate, into spiritual channels; to turn natural anger into spiritual zeal, natural mirth into holy cheerfulness, and natural fear into a holy dread and awe of God. This method of cure Christ prescribes in the tenth of Matthew; similar to which is Isaiah 8:12, 13, 'Fear not their fear.' But how shall we help it? 'Sanctify the Lord of hosts himself; and let him be your fear, and let him be your dread.' Natural fear may be allayed for the present by natural reason, or the removal of the occasion; but then

it is like a candle blown out by a puff of breath, which is easily blown in again: but if the fear of God extinguish it, then it is like a candle quenched in water, which cannot easily be rekindled.

14. Pour out to God in prayer those fears which the devil and your own unbelief pour in upon you in times of danger. Prayer is the best outlet to fear: where is the Christian that cannot set his seal to this direction? I will give you the greatest example to encourage you to compliance, even the example of Jesus Christ. When the hour of his danger and death drew nigh, he went into the garden, separated from his disciples, and there wrestled mightily with God in prayer, even unto agony; in reference to which the apostle says, 'who in the days of his flesh, when he had offered up prayers and supplications, with strong cries and tears, to him that was able to save from death, and was heard in that he feared.' He was heard as to strength and support to carry him through it; though not as to deliverance, or exemption from it. Oh that these things may abide with you, and be reduced to practice in these evil days, and that many trembling souls may be established by them.

The *fifth season*, requiring diligence in keeping the heart, is the time of *outward wants*. Although at such times we should complain *to* God, not *of* God (the throne of grace being erected for a 'time of need'), yet when the waters of relief run low, and want begins to press, how prone are the best hearts to distrust the fountain! When the meal in the barrel and the oil in the cruse are almost spent, our faith and patience too are almost spent. It is now difficult to keep the proud and unbelieving heart in a holy quietude and sweet submission at the foot of God. It is an easy thing to talk of trusting God for daily bread, while we have a full barn or purse; but to say as the prophet, 'Though the fig-tree should not blossom, neither fruit be in the vine.... yet will I rejoice in the Lord...', surely this is not easy.

Would you know then how a Christian may keep his heart from distrusting God, or repining against him, when outward wants are either felt or feared? – The case deserves to be seriously considered, especially now, since it seems to be the design of Providence to empty the people of God of their creature fullness, and acquaint them with those difficulties to which hitherto they have been altogether strangers. To secure the heart from the dangers attending this condition, these considerations may, through the blessing of the Spirit, prove effectual:

1. If God reduces you to necessities, he therein deals no otherwise with you than he has done with some of the holiest men that ever lived. Your condition is not singular; though you have hitherto been a stranger to want, other saints have been familiarly acquainted with it. Hear what Paul says, not of himself only, but in the name of other saints reduced to like exigencies: 'Even to the present hour, we both hunger and thirst, and are naked, and are buffeted, and have no certain dwelling-place.' To see such a man as *Paul* going up and down the world naked, and hungry, and houseless; one that was so far above thee in grace and holiness; one that did more service for God in a day than perhaps thou hast done in all thy days may well put an end to your repining. Have you forgotten how much even a David has suffered? How great were his difficulties! 'Give, I pray thee,' says he to Nabal, 'whatsoever cometh to

thy hand, to thy servants, and to thy son David.' But why speak I of these? Behold a greater than any of them, even the Son of God, *who is the heir of all things, and by whom the worlds were made,* sometimes would have been glad of any thing, having nothing to eat. 'And on the morrow, when they were come from Bethany, he was hungry; and seeing a fig-tree afar off, having leaves, he came, if haply he might find any thing thereon.'

Hereby then God has set no mark of hatred upon you, neither can you infer want of *love* from want of *bread*. When thy repining heart puts the question, 'Was there ever sorrow like unto mine?' ask these worthies, and they will tell thee that though they did not complain as thou dost, yet their condition was as necessitous as thine is.

2. If God leave you not in this condition without a promise, you have no reason to repine or despond under it. That is a sad condition indeed to which no promise belongs. Calvin in his comment on Isaiah 9:1, explains in what sense the darkness of the captivity was not so great as that of the lesser incursions made by Tiglath Pileser. In the captivity, the city was destroyed and the temple burnt with fire: there was no comparison in the *affliction,* yet the *darkness* was not so great, because, says he, 'there was a certain *promise* made in this case, but none in the other'. It is better to be as low as hell *with* a promise, than to be in paradise *without* one. Even the darkness of hell itself would be no darkness comparatively at all, were there but a promise to enlighten it.

Now, God has left many sweet promises for the faith of his poor people to live upon in this condition; such as these: 'Oh fear the Lord, ye his saints, for there is no want to them that fear him; the lions do lack and suffer hunger, but they that fear the Lord shall not want any good thing.' 'The eye of the Lord is upon the righteous to keep them alive in famine.' 'No good thing will he withhold from them that walk uprightly.' 'He that spared not his own Son, but delivered him up for us all, how shall he not with him also freely give us all things?' 'When the poor and the needy seek water, and there is none, and their tongue faileth for thirst, I the Lord will hear them, I the God of Israel will not forsake them.' Here you see their extreme wants, water being put for their necessaries of life; and their certain relief, 'I the Lord will hear them'; in which it is supposed that they cry unto him in their distress, and he hears their cry. Having therefore these promises, why should not your distrustful heart conclude like David's, 'The Lord is my shepherd, I shall not want?'

'But these promises imply conditions: if they were absolute, they would afford more satisfaction.' What are those tacit conditions of which you speak but these, that he will either supply or sanctify your wants; that you shall have so much as God sees fit for you? And does this trouble you? Would you have the mercy, whether sanctified or not? whether God sees it fit for you or not? The appetites of saints after earthly things should not be so ravenous as to seize greedily upon any enjoyment without regarding circumstances.

'But when wants press, and I see not whence supplies should come, my faith in the promise shakes, and I, like murmuring Israel, cry, 'He gave bread, can he give water also?' O unbelieving heart! When did his promises fail? Who ever trusted them and was ashamed? May not God upbraid thee with thine unreasonable infidelity, as in Jeremiah 2:31, 'Have I been a wilderness unto you?' or as

Christ said to his disciples, 'Since I was with you, lacked ye any thing?' Yea, may you not upbraid yourself; may you not say with good old Polycarp, 'These many years I have served Christ, and found him a good Master'?

Indeed he may deny what your *wantonness*, but not what your *want* calls for. He will not regard the cry of your *lusts*, nor yet despise the cry of your *faith:* though he will not indulge your *wanton appetites*, yet he will not violate his own *faithful promises.* These promises are your best security for *eternal life;* and it is strange they should not satisfy you for daily *bread.* Remember the words of the Lord, and solace your heart with them amidst all your wants. It is said of Epicurus, that in dreadful paroxysms of the cholic he often refreshed himself by calling to mind his inventions in philosophy; and of Posidonius the philosopher, that in an acute disorder he solaced himself with discourses on moral virtue; and when distressed, he would say, 'O pain, thou dost nothing; though thou art a little troublesome, I will never confess thee to be evil.' If upon such grounds as these they could support themselves under such racking pains, and even deluded their diseases by them; how much rather should the promises of God, and the sweet experiences which have gone along step by step with them, make you forget all your wants, and comfort you in every difficulty?

3. If it be bad now, it might have been worse. Has God denied thee the comforts of this life? He might have denied thee Christ, peace, and pardon also; and then thy case had been woeful indeed.

You know God has done so to millions. How many such wretched objects may your eyes behold every day, that have no comfort in hand, nor yet in hope; that are miserable here, and will be so to eternity; that have a bitter cup, and nothing to sweeten it – no, not so much as any hope that it will be better. But it is not so with you: though you be poor in this world, yet you are 'rich in faith, an heir of the kingdom which God has promised'. Learn to set spiritual riches over against temporal poverty. Balance all your present troubles with your spiritual privileges. Indeed if God has denied your soul the robe of righteousness to *clothe* it, the hidden manna to *feed* it, the heavenly mansion to *receive* it, you might well be pensive; but the consideration that he has not may administer comfort under any outward distress. When Luther began to be pressed by want, he said, 'Let us be contented with our hard fare; for do not we feast upon Christ, the bread of life?' 'Blessed be God,' said Paul, 'who hath abounded to us in all spiritual blessings.'

4. Though this affliction be great, God has far greater, with which he chastises the dearly beloved of his soul in this world. Should he remove this and inflict those, you would account your present state a very comfortable one, and bless God to be as you now are. Should God remove your present troubles, supply all your outward wants, give you the desire of your heart in creature-comforts; but hide his face from you, shoot his arrows into your soul, and cause the venom of them to drink up your spirit: should he leave you but a few days to the buffetings of Satan: should he hold your eyes but a few nights waking with horrors of conscience, tossing to and fro till the dawning of the day: – should he lead you through the chambers of death, show you the visions of darkness, and make his terrors set themselves in array against you: then tell me if you would not think it a great mercy to be back again in your former necessitous condition with peace of conscience; and account bread and water, with God's favour,

a happy state? Oh then take heed of repining. Say not that God deals hardly with you, lest you provoke him to convince you by your own sense that he has worse rods than these for unsubmissive and froward children.

5. If it be bad now, it will be better shortly. Keep thy heart by this consideration, 'the meal in the barrel is almost spent; well, be it so, why should that trouble me, if I am almost beyond the need and use of these things?' The traveller has spent almost all his money; 'well,' says he, 'though my money be almost spent, my journey is almost finished too: I am near home, and shall soon be fully supplied.' If there be no candles in the house, it is a comfort to think that it is almost day, and then there will be no need of them. I am afraid, Christian, you misreckon when you think your provision is almost spent, and you have a great way to travel, many years to live and nothing to live upon; it may be not half so many as you suppose. In this be confident, if your provision be spent, either fresh supplies are coming, though you see not whence, or you are nearer your journey's end than you reckon yourself to be. Desponding soul, does it become a man travelling upon the road to that heavenly city, and almost arrived there, within a few days' journey of his Father's house, where all his wants shall be supplied, to be so anxious about a little meat, or drink, or clothes, which he fears he shall want by the way? It was nobly said by the forty martyrs when turned out naked in a frosty night to be starved to death, 'The winter indeed is sharp and cold, but heaven is warm and comfortable; here we shiver for cold, but Abraham's bosom will make amends for all.'

'But,' says the desponding soul, 'I may die for want.' Who ever did so? When were the righteous forsaken? If indeed it be so, your journey is ended, and you fully supplied.

'But I am not sure of that; were I sure of heaven, it would be another matter.' Are you not sure of that? Then you have other matters to trouble yourself about than these; methinks these should be the least of all your cares. I do not find that souls perplexed about the want of Christ, pardon of sin, etc. are usually very solicitous about these things. He that seriously puts such questions as these, 'What shall I do to be saved? How shall I know my sin is pardoned?' does not trouble himself with, 'What shall I eat, what shall I drink, or wherewithal shall I be clothed?'

6. Does it become the children of such a Father to distrust his all-sufficiency, or repine at any of his dispensations? Do you well to question his care and love upon every new exigency? Say, have you not formerly been ashamed of this? Has not your Father's seasonable provision for you in former difficulties put you to the blush, and made you resolve never more to question his love and care? And yet will you again renew your unworthy suspicions of him? Disingenuous child! Reason thus with yourself: 'If I perish for want of what is good and needful for me, it must be either because my Father knows not my wants, or has not wherewith to supply them, or regards not what becomes of me. Which of these shall I charge upon him? Not the first: for *my Father knows what I have need of.* Not the second: for *the earth is the Lord's and the fullness thereof;* his *name is God all-sufficient.* Not the last: for *as a Father pitieth his children, so the Lord pitieth them that fear him; the Lord is exceeding pitiful and of tender mercy; he hears the young ravens when they cry:* and will he not hear me? *Consider,* says Christ, *the fowls of the air;* not the fowls at the door that are fed every day by hand, but the fowls of the air that have none to provide

for them. Does he feed and clothe his enemies, and will he forget his children? He heard even the cry of Ishmael in distress. Oh my unbelieving heart, dost thou yet doubt?'

7. Your poverty is not your sin, but your affliction. If you have not by sinful means brought it upon yourself, and if it be but an affliction, it may the more easily be borne. It is hard indeed to bear an affliction coming upon us as the fruit and punishment of sin. When men are under trouble upon that account; they say, 'O if it were but a single affliction, coming from the hand of God by way of trial, I could bear it; but I have brought it upon myself by sin, it comes as the punishment of sin; the marks of God's displeasure are upon it: it is the guilt within that troubles and galls more than the want without.' But it is not so here; therefore you have no reason to be cast down under it.

'But though there be no sting of guilt, yet this condition wants not other stings; as, for instance, the discredit of religion. I cannot comply with my engagements in the world, and thereby religion is likely to suffer.' It is well you have a heart to discharge every duty; yet if God disable you by providence, it is no discredit to your profession that you do not that which you cannot do, so long as it is your desire and endeavour to do what you can and ought to do; and in this case God's will is, that lenity and forbearance be exercised toward you.

'But it grieves me to behold the necessities of others, whom I was wont to relieve and refresh, but now cannot.' If you cannot, it ceases to be your duty, and God accepts the drawing out of your soul to the hungry in compassion and desire to help them, though you cannot draw forth a full purse to relieve and supply them.

'But I find such a condition full of temptations, a great hindrance in the way to heaven.' Every condition in the world has its hindrances and attending temptations; and were you in a prosperous condition, you might there meet with more temptations and fewer advantages than you now have; for though I confess poverty as well as prosperity has its temptations, yet I am confident prosperity has not those advantages that poverty has. Here you have an opportunity to discover the sincerity of your love to God, when you can live upon him, find enough in him, and constantly follow him, even when all external inducements and motives fail.

Thus I have shown you how to keep your heart from the temptations and dangers attending a low condition in the world. When want oppresses and the heart begins to sink, then improve, and bless God for these helps to keep it.

The *sixth season* requiring this diligence in keeping the heart, is the *season of duty*. Our hearts must be closely watched and kept when we draw nigh to God in public, private, or secret duties; for the vanity of the heart seldom discovers itself more than at such times. How often does the poor soul cry out, 'Oh Lord, how gladly would I serve thee, but vain thoughts will not let me: I come to open my heart to thee, to delight my soul in communion with thee, but my corruptions oppose me: Lord, call off these vain thoughts, and suffer them not to estrange the soul that is espoused to thee.'

The question then is this: how may the heart be kept from distractions by vain thoughts in time of duty?

There is a two-fold distraction, or wandering of the heart in duty: first, voluntary and habitual, 'They set not their hearts aright, and their spirit was not steadfast with

God.' This is the case of formalists, and it proceeds from the want of a holy inclination of the heart to God; their hearts are under the power of their lusts, and therefore it is no wonder that they go after their lusts, even when they are about holy things.

Secondly, involuntary and lamented distractions: 'I find then a law, that when I would do good, evil is present with me; Oh wretched man that I am...' This proceeds not from the want of a holy inclination or aim, but from the weakness of grace and the want of vigilance in opposing indwelling sin. But it is not my business to show you how these distractions come into the heart, but rather how to get them out, and prevent their future admission:

1. Sequester yourself from all earthly employments, and set apart some time for solemn preparation to meet God in duty. You cannot come directly from the world into God's presence without finding a savour of the world in your duties. It is with the heart (a few minutes since plunged in the world, now in the presence of God) as it is with the sea after a storm, which still continues working, muddy and disquiet, though the wind be laid and the storm be over. Your heart must have some time to settle. Few musicians can take an instrument and play upon it without some time and labour to tune it; few Christians can say with David, 'My heart is fixed, Oh God, it is fixed.' When you go to God in any duty, take your heart aside and say, 'Oh my soul, I am now engaged in the greatest work that a creature was ever employed about; I am going into the awful presence of God upon business of everlasting moment. Oh my soul, leave trifling now; be composed, be watchful, be serious; this is no common work, it is soul-work; it is work for eternity;

it is work which will bring forth fruit to life or death in the world to come.' Pause awhile and consider your sins, your wants, your troubles; keep your thoughts awhile on these before you address yourself to duty. David first mused, and then spake with his tongue.

2. Having composed your heart by previous meditation, immediately set a guard upon your senses. How often are Christians in danger of losing the eyes of their mind by those of their body! Against this David prayed, 'Turn away mine eyes from beholding vanity, and quicken thou me in thy way.' This may serve to expound the Arabian proverb: 'Shut the windows that the house may be light.' It were well if you could say in the commencement, as a holy man once said when he came from the performance of duty: 'Be shut, Oh my eyes, be shut; for it is impossible that you should ever discern such beauty and glory in any creature as I have now seen in God.' You must avoid all occasions of distraction from without, and imbibe that intenseness of spirit in the work of God which locks up the eye and ear against vanity.

3. Beg of God a mortified fancy. 'A working fancy,' saith one, 'how much soever it be extolled among men, is a great snare to the soul, except it work in fellowship with right reason and a sanctified heart. 'The fancy is a power of the soul, placed between the senses and the understanding; it is that which first stirs itself in the soul, and by its motions the other powers of the soul are brought into exercise; it is that in which thoughts are first formed, and as that is, so are they. If imaginations be not first cast down, it is impossible that every thought of the heart should be brought into obedience to Christ. The fancy is naturally the wildest and most untameable power of the soul. Some Christians have

much to do with it; and the more spiritual the heart is, the more does a wild and vain fancy disturb and perplex it. It is a sad thing that one's imagination should call off the soul from attending on God, when it is engaged in communion with him. Pray earnestly and perseveringly that your fancy may be chastened and sanctified, and when this is accomplished your thoughts will be regular and fixed.

4. If you would keep your heart from vain excursions when engaged in duties, realize to yourself, by faith, the holy and awful presence of God. If the presence of a grave man would compose you to seriousness, how much more should the presence of a holy God? Do you think that you would dare to be gay and light if you realized the presence and inspection of the Divine Being? Remember where you are when engaged in religious duty, and act as if you believed in the omniscience of God. 'All things are naked and open to the eyes of Him with whom we have to do.' Realize his infinite holiness, his purity, his spirituality.

Strive to obtain such apprehensions of the greatness of God as shall suitably affect your heart; and remember his jealousy over his worship. 'This is that the Lord spake, saying, I will be sanctified in them that come nigh me, and before all the people I will be glorified.' 'A man that is praying,' says Bernard, 'should behave himself as if he were entering into the court of heaven, where he sees the Lord upon his throne, surrounded with ten thousand of his angels and saints ministering unto him.'

When you come from an exercise in which your heart has been wandering and listless, what can you say? Suppose all the vanities and impertinences which have passed through your mind during a devotional exercise were written down and interlined with your petitions, could you have the face to present them to God? Should your tongue utter all the thoughts of your heart when attending the worship of God, would not men abhor you? Yet your thoughts are perfectly known to God. O think upon this scripture: 'God is greatly to be feared in the assemblies of his saints, and to be had in reverence of all them that are round about him.' Why did the Lord descend in thunderings and lightnings and dark clouds upon Sinai? Why did the mountains smoke under him, the people quake and tremble round about him, Moses himself not excepted? but to teach the people this great truth: 'Let us have grace, whereby we may serve him acceptably, with reverence and godly fear; for our God is a consuming fire.' Such apprehensions of the character and presence of God will quickly reduce a heart inclined to vanity to a more serious frame.

5. Maintain a prayerful frame of heart in the intervals of duty. What reason can be assigned why our hearts are so dull, so careless, so wandering, when we hear or pray, but that there have been long intermissions in our communion with God? If that divine unction, that spiritual fervour, and those holy impressions, which we obtain from God while engaged in the performance of one duty, were preserved to enliven and engage us in the performance of another, they would be of incalculable service to keep our hearts serious and devout. For this purpose, frequent ejaculations between stated and solemn duties are of most excellent use: they not only preserve the mind in a composed and pious frame, but they connect one stated duty, as it were, with another, and keep the attention of the soul alive to all its interests and obligations.

6. If you would have the distraction of your thoughts prevented, endeavour to raise your affections to God, and to engage them warmly in your duty. When the soul is intent upon any work, it gathers in its strength and bends all its thoughts to that work; and when it is deeply affected, it will pursue its object with intenseness; the affections will gain an ascendancy over the thoughts and guide them. But deadness causes distraction, and distraction increases deadness. Could you but regard your duties as the medium in which you might walk in communion with God, in which your soul might be filled with those ravishing and matchless delights which his presence affords, you might have no inclination to neglect them. But if you would prevent the recurrence of distracting thoughts, if you would find your happiness in the performance of duty, you must not only be careful that you engage in what is your duty, but labour with patient and persevering exertion to interest your feelings in it. Why is your heart so inconstant, especially in secret duties; why are you ready to be gone, almost as soon as you are come into the presence of God, but because your affections are not engaged?

7. When you are disturbed by vain thoughts, humble yourself before God, and call in assistance from heaven. When the messenger of Satan buffeted St Paul by wicked suggestions, (as is supposed) he mourned before God on account of it. Never slight wandering thoughts in duty as small matters; follow every such thought with a deep regret. Turn to God with such words as these: 'Lord, I came hither to commune with thee, and here a busy adversary and a vain heart, conspiring together, have opposed me. Oh my God! what a heart have I! Shall I never wait upon thee without

distraction? When shall I enjoy an hour of free communion with thee? Grant me thine assistance at this time; discover thy glory to me, and my heart will quickly be recovered. I came hither to enjoy thee, and shall I go away without thee? Behold my distress, and help me!'– Could you but sufficiently bewail your distractions, and repair to God for deliverance from them, you would gain relief.

8. Look upon the success and the comfort of your duties, as depending very much upon the keeping of your heart close with God in them. These two things, the success of duty and the inward comfort arising from the performance of it, are unspeakably dear to the Christian; but both of these will be lost if the heart be in a listless state. 'Surely God heareth not vanity, nor doth the Almighty regard it.' The promise is made to a heart engaged: 'Then shall ye seek for me, and find me, when ye shall search for me with all your heart.' When you find your heart under the power of deadness and distraction, say to yourself, 'Oh what do I lose by a careless heart now! My praying seasons are the most valuable portions of my life: could I but raise my heart to God, I might now obtain such mercies as would be matter of praise to all eternity.'

9. Regard your carefulness or carelessness in this matter as a great evidence of your sincerity, or hypocrisy. Nothing will alarm an upright heart more than this. 'What! shall I give way to a customary wandering of the heart from God? Shall the spot of the hypocrite appear upon my soul? Hypocrites, indeed, can drudge on in the round of duty, never regarding the frame of their hearts; but shall I do so? Never – never let me be satisfied with empty duties. Never

let me take my leave of a duty until my eyes have seen the King, the Lord of Hosts.'

10. It will be of special use to keep your heart with God in duty, to consider what influence all your duties will have upon your eternity. Your religious seasons are your seed times, and in another world you must reap the fruits of what you sow in your duties here. If you sow to the flesh, you will reap corruption; if you sow to the Spirit, you will reap life everlasting. Answer seriously these questions: Are you willing to reap the fruit of vanity in the world to come? Dare you say, when your thoughts are roving to the ends of the earth in duty, when you scarce mind what you say or hear, 'Now, Lord, I am sowing to the Spirit; now I am providing and laying up for eternity; now I am seeking for glory, honour and immortality; now I am striving to enter in at the strait gate; now I am taking the kingdom of heaven by holy violence!' Such reflections are well calculated to dissipate vain thoughts.

The *seventh season*, which requires more than common diligence to keep the heart, is *when we receive injuries and abuses from men.* Such is the depravity and corruption of man, that one is become as a wolf or a tiger to another. And as men are naturally cruel and oppressive one to another, so the wicked conspire to abuse and wrong the people of God, 'The wicked devoureth the man that is more righteous than he.' Now when we are thus abused and wronged, it is hard to keep the heart from revengeful motions; to make it meekly and quietly commit the cause to him that judgeth righteously; to prevent the exercise of any sinful affection. The spirit that is in us lusteth to revenge; but it must not be so. We have choice helps in the gospel to keep our hearts from sinful motions against our enemies, and to sweeten our embittered spirits. Do you ask how a Christian may keep his heart from revengeful motions under the greatest injuries and abuses from men? I reply: When you find your heart begin to be inflamed by revengeful feelings, immediately reflect on the following things:

1. Urge upon your heart the severe prohibitions of revenge contained in the law of God. However gratifying to your corrupt propensities revenge may be, remember that it is forbidden. Hear the word of God: 'Say not, I will recompense evil.' Say not, I will do so to him as he hath done to me. 'Recompense to no man evil for evil. Avenge not yourselves, but give place unto wrath; for it is written, Vengeance is mine, I will repay, saith the Lord.' On the contrary. 'If thine enemy hunger, feed him; if he thirst, give him drink.' It was an argument urged by the Christians to prove their religion to be supernatural and pure, that it forbids revenge, which is so agreeable to nature; and it is to be wished that such an argument might not be laid aside. Awe your heart, then, with the authority of God in the Scriptures; and when carnal reason says, 'My enemy deserves to be hated,' let conscience reply, 'But doth God deserve to be disobeyed?' 'Thus and thus hath he done, and so hath he wronged me'; 'But what hath God done that I should wrong him? If my enemy dares boldly to break the peace, shall I be so wicked as to break the precept? If he fears not to wrong me, shall not I fear to wrong God?' Thus let the fear of God restrain and calm your feelings.

2. Set before your eyes the most eminent patterns of meekness and forgiveness, that you may feel the force of their example. This is the way to cut off the common pleas of

flesh and blood for revenge: as thus, 'No man would bear such an affront'; yes, others have borne as bad, and worse ones. 'But I shall be reckoned a coward, a fool, if I pass by this': no matter, so long as you follow the examples of the wisest and holiest of men. Never did any one suffer more or greater abuses from men than Jesus did, nor did any one ever endure insult and reproach and every kind of abuse in a more peaceful and forgiving manner; when he was reviled he reviled not again; when he suffered, he threatened not; when his murderers crucified him he prayed, *Father, forgive them*; and herein he hath set us an example, that we should follow his steps. Thus his apostles imitated him: 'Being reviled,' say they, 'we bless; being persecuted, we suffer it; being defamed, we entreat.' I have often heard it reported of the holy Mr Dod, that when a man, enraged at his close, convincing doctrine, assaulted him, smote him on the face and dashed out two of his teeth; that meek servant of Christ spit out the teeth and blood into his hand, and said, 'See here, you have knocked out two of my teeth, and that without any just provocation; but on condition that I might do your soul good, I would give you leave to knock out all the rest.' Here was exemplified the excellency of the Christian spirit. Strive then for this spirit, which constitutes the true excellence of Christians. Do what others cannot do, keep this spirit in exercise, and you will preserve peace in your own soul and gain the victory over your enemies.

3. Consider the character of the person who has wronged you. He is either a good or a wicked man. If he is a good man, there is light and tenderness in his conscience, which sooner or later will bring him to a sense of the evil of what he has done. If he is a good man, Christ has forgiven him

greater injuries than he has done to you; and why should not you forgive him? Will Christ not upbraid him for any of his wrongs, but frankly forgive them all; and will you take him by the throat for some petty abuse which he has offered you?

4. But if a wicked man has injured or insulted you, truly you have more reason to exercise pity than revenge toward him. He is in a deluded and miserable state; a slave to sin and an enemy to righteousness. If he should ever repent, he will be ready to make you reparation; if he continues impenitent, there is a day coming when he will be punished to the extent of his deserts. You need not study revenge; God will execute vengeance upon him.

5. Remember that by revenge you can only gratify a sinful passion, which by forgiveness you might conquer. Suppose that by revenge you might destroy one enemy; yet, by exercising the Christian's temper you might conquer three – your own lust, Satan's temptation, and your enemy's heart. If by revenge you should overcome your enemy, the victory would be unhappy and inglorious, for in gaining it you would be overcome by your own corruption; but by exercising a meek and forgiving temper, you will always come off with honour and success. It must be a very disingenuous nature indeed upon which meekness and forgiveness will not operate; that must be a flinty heart which this fire will not melt. Thus David gained such a victory over Saul his persecutor, that 'Saul lifted up his voice and wept, and he said to David, Thou art more righteous than I.'

6. Seriously propose this question to your own heart: 'Have I got any good by means of the wrongs and injuries which

I have received?' If they have done you no good, turn your revenge upon yourself. You have reason to be filled with shame and sorrow that you should have a heart which can deduce no good from such trouble; that your temper should be so unlike that of Christ. The patience and meekness of other Christians have turned all the injuries offered to them to a good account; their souls have been animated to praise God when they have been loaded with reproaches from the world. 'I thank my God,' said Jerome, 'that I am worthy to be hated of the world.' But if you have derived any benefit from the reproaches and wrongs which you have received, if they have put you upon examining your own heart, if they have made you more careful how you conduct, if they have convinced you of the value of a sanctified temper; will you not forgive them? Will you not forgive one who has been instrumental of so much good to you? What though he meant it for evil? If through the Divine blessing your happiness has been promoted by what he has done, why should you even have a hard thought of him?

7. Consider by whom all your troubles are ordered. This will be of great use to keep your heart from revenge; this will quickly calm and sweeten your temper. When Shimei railed at David and cursed him, the spirit of that good man was not at all poisoned by revenge; for when Abishai offered him, if he pleased, the head of Shimei, the king said, 'Let him curse, because the Lord hath said unto him, Curse David: who shall then say, Wherefore hast thou done so?' It may be that God uses him as his rod to chastise me, because by my sin I gave the enemies of God occasion to blaspheme; and shall I be angry with the instrument? How irrational were that! Thus Job was quieted; he did not rail and meditate revenge upon the Chaldeans and Sabeans,

but regarded God as the orderer of his troubles, and said, 'The Lord hath taken away, blessed be his name.'

8. Consider how you are daily and hourly wronging God, and you will not be so easily inflamed with revenge against those who have wronged you. You are constantly affronting God, yet he does not take vengeance on you, but bears with you and forgives; and will you rise up and avenge yourself upon others? Reflect on this cutting rebuke: 'Oh thou wicked and slothful servant! I forgave thee all that debt because thou desiredst me; shouldst thou not also have compassion on thy fellow-servant, even as I had pity on thee?' None should be so filled with forbearance and mercy to such as wrong them, as those who have experienced the riches of mercy themselves. The mercy of God to us should melt our hearts into mercy toward others. It is impossible that we should be cruel to others, except we forget how kind and compassionate God hath been to us. And if kindness cannot prevail in us, methinks fear should: 'If ye forgive not men their trespasses, neither will your Father forgive your trespasses.'

9. Let the consideration that the day of the Lord draweth nigh restrain you from anticipating it by acts of revenge. Why are you so hasty? Is not the Lord at hand to avenge all his abused servants? 'Be patient therefore, brethren, unto the coming of the Lord. Behold, the husbandman waiteth…. Be ye also patient, for the coming of the Lord draweth nigh. Grudge not one against another, brethren, lest ye be condemned. Behold, the Judge standeth at the door.' Vengeance belongeth unto God, and will you wrong yourself so much as to assume his work?

The next season in which special exertion is necessary to keep the heart, is when we meet with *great trials*. In such cases the heart is apt to be suddenly transported with pride, impatience, or other sinful passions. Many good people are guilty of hasty and very sinful conduct in such instances; and all have need to use diligently the following means to keep their hearts submissive and patient under great trials:

1. Get humble and abasing thoughts of yourself. The humble is ever the patient man. Pride is the source of irregular and sinful passions. A lofty, will be an unyielding and peevish spirit. When we over-rate ourselves, we think that we are treated unworthily, that our trials are too severe: thus we cavil and repine. Christian, you should have such thoughts of yourself as would put a stop to these murmurings. You should have lower and more humiliating views of yourself than any other one can have of you. Get humility, and you will have peace whatever be your trial.

2. Cultivate a habit of communion with God. This will prepare you for whatever may take place. This will so sweeten your temper and calm your mind as to secure you against surprisals. This will produce that inward peace which will make you superior to your trials. Habitual communion with God will afford you enjoyment, which you can never be willing to interrupt by sinful feeling. When a Christian is calm and submissive under his afflictions, probably he derives support and comfort in this way; but he who is discomposed, impatient, or fretful, shows that all is not right within – he cannot be supposed to practise communion with God.

3. Let your mind be deeply impressed with an apprehension of the evil nature and effects of an unsubmissive and restless

temper. It grieves the Spirit of God, and induces his departure. His gracious presence and influence are enjoyed only where peace and quiet submission prevail. The indulgence of such a temper gives the adversary an advantage. Satan is an angry and discontented spirit. He finds no rest but in restless hearts. He bestirs himself when the spirits are in commotion; sometimes he fills the heart with ungrateful and rebellious thoughts; sometimes he inflames the tongue with indecent language. Again, such a temper brings great guilt upon the conscience, unfits the soul for any duty, and dishonours the Christian name. O keep your heart, and let the power and excellence of your religion be chiefly manifested when you are brought into the greatest straits.

4. Consider how desirable it is for a Christian to overcome his evil propensities. How much more present happiness it affords; how much better it is in every respect to mortify and subdue unholy feelings, than to give way to them. When upon your deathbed you come calmly to review your life, how comfortable will it be to reflect on the conquest which you have made over the depraved feelings of your heart. It was a memorable saying of Valentinian the emperor, when he was about to die: 'Amongst all my conquests, there is but one that now comforts me.' Being asked what that was, he answered, 'I have overcome my worst enemy, my own sinful heart!'

5. Shame yourself, by contemplating the character of those who have been most eminent for meekness and submission. Above all, compare your temper with the Spirit of Christ. 'Learn of me,' saith he, 'for I am meek and lowly.' It is said of Calvin and Ursin, though both of choleric natures, that they had so imbibed and cultivated the meekness

of Christ as not to utter an unbecoming word under the greatest provocations. And even many of the heathens have manifested great moderation and forbearance under their severest afflictions. Is it not a shame and a reproach that you should be outdone by them?

6. Avoid every thing which is calculated to irritate your feelings. It is true spiritual valour to keep as far as we can out of sin's way. If you can but avoid the excitements to impetuous and rebellious feelings, or check them in their first beginnings, you will have but little to fear. The first workings of common sins are comparatively weak, they gain their strength by degrees; but in times of trial the motions of sin are strongest at first, the unsubdued temper breaks out suddenly and violently. But if you resolutely withstand it at first, it will yield and give you the victory.

The *ninth season* wherein the greatest diligence and skill are necessary to keep the heart, is the hour of *temptation*, when Satan besets the Christian's heart, and takes the unwary by surprise. To keep the heart at such times, is not less a mercy than a duty. Few Christians are so skilful in detecting the fallacies, and repelling the arguments by which the adversary incites them to sin, as to come off safe and whole in these encounters. Many eminent saints have smarted severely for their want of watchfulness and diligence at such times. How then may a Christian keep his heart from yielding to temptation? There are several principal ways in which the adversary insinuates temptation, and urges compliance:

1. Satan suggests that here is pleasure to be enjoyed; the temptation is presented with a smiling aspect and an

enticing voice: 'What, are you so dull and phlegmatic as not to feel the powerful charms of pleasure? Who can withhold himself from such delights?' Reader, you may be rescued from the danger of such temptations by repelling the proposal of pleasure. It is urged that the commission of sin will afford you pleasure. Suppose this were true, will the accusing and condemning rebukes of conscience and the flames of hell be pleasant too? Is there pleasure in the scourges of conscience? If so, why did Peter weep so bitterly? Why did David cry out of broken bones? You hear what is said of the pleasure of sin, and have you not read what David said of the effects of it? 'Thine arrows stick fast in me, and thy hand presseth me sore; there is no soundness in my flesh because of thine anger, neither is there any rest in my bones because of my sin...' If you yield to temptation, you must feel such inward distress on account of it, or the miseries of hell. But why should the pretended pleasure of sin allure you, when you know that unspeakably more real pleasure will arise from the mortification than can arise from the commission of sin? Will you prefer the gratification of some unhallowed passion, with the deadly poison which it will leave behind, to that sacred pleasure which arises from fearing and obeying God, complying with the dictates of conscience, and maintaining inward peace? Can sin afford any such delight as he feels who, by resisting temptation, has manifested the sincerity of his heart, and obtained evidence that he fears God, loves holiness, and hates sin?

2. The secrecy with which you may commit sin is made use of to induce compliance with temptation. The tempter insinuates that this indulgence will never disgrace you among men, for no one will know it. But recollect yourself.

Does not God behold you? Is not the divine presence everywhere? What if you might hide your sin from the eyes of the world, you cannot hide it from God. No darkness nor shadow of death can screen you from his inspection. Besides, have you no reverence for yourself? Can you do that by yourself which you dare not have others observe? Is not your conscience as a thousand witnesses? Even a heathen could say, 'When thou art tempted to commit sin, fear thyself without any other witness.'

3. The prospect of worldly advantage often enforces temptation. It is suggested, 'Why should you be so nice and scrupulous? Give yourself a little liberty, and you may better your condition: now is your time.' This is a dangerous temptation, and must be promptly resisted. Yielding to such a temptation will do your soul more injury than any temporal acquisition can possibly do you good. And what would it profit you, if you should gain the whole world and lose your own soul? What can be compared with the value of your spiritual interests? Or what can at all compensate for the smallest injury of them?

4. Perhaps the smallness of the sin is urged as a reason why you may commit it; thus: 'It is but a little one, a small matter, a trifle; who would stand upon such niceties?' But is the Majesty of heaven little too? If you commit this sin you will offend a great God. Is there any little hell to torment little sinners in? No; the least sinners in hell are full of misery. There is great wrath treasured up for those whom the world regard as little sinners. But the less the sin, the less the inducement to commit it. Will you provoke God for a trifle? Will you destroy your peace, wound your conscience, and grieve the Spirit, all for nothing? What madness is this!

5. An argument to enforce temptation is sometimes drawn from the mercy of God and the hope of pardon – God is merciful, he will pass by this as an infirmity, he will not be severe to mark it. But stay: where do you find a promise of mercy to presumptuous sinners? Involuntary reprisals and lamented infirmities may be pardoned, 'but the soul that doth aught presumptuously, the same reproacheth the Lord, and that soul shall be cut off from among his people.' If God is a being of so much mercy, how can you affront him? How can you make so glorious an attribute as the divine mercy an occasion of sin? Will you wrong him because he is good? Rather let his goodness lead you to repentance, and keep you from transgression.

6. Sometimes Satan encourages to the commission of sin, from the examples of holy men. Thus and thus they sinned, and were restored; therefore you may commit this sin, and yet be a saint and be saved. Such suggestions must be instantly repelled. If good men have committed sins similar to that with which you are beset, did any good man ever sin upon such ground and from such encouragement as is here presented? Did God cause their examples to be recorded for your imitation, or for your warning? Are they not set up as beacons that you may avoid the rocks upon which they split? Are you willing to feel what they felt for sin? Dare you follow them in sin, and plunge yourself into such distress and danger as they incurred?– Reader, in these ways learn to keep your heart in the hour of temptation.

The time of *doubting and of spiritual darkness* constitutes another season when it is very difficult to keep the heart. When the light and comfort of the divine presence is withdrawn; when the believer, from the prevalence of indwelling sin in one form or other, is ready to renounce his hopes, to infer desperate conclusions with respect to himself, to regard his former comforts as vain delusions, and his professions as hypocrisy; at such a time much diligence is necessary to keep the heart from despondency.

The Christian's distress arises from his apprehension of his spiritual state, and in general he argues against his possessing true religion, either from his having relapsed into the same sins from which he had formerly been recovered with shame and sorrow; or from the sensible declining of his affections from God; or from the strength of his affections toward creature enjoyments; or from his enlargement in public, while he is often confined and barren in private duties; or from some horrible suggestions of Satan, with which his soul is greatly perplexed; or, lastly, from God's silence and seeming denial of his long-depending prayers.

Now in order to the establishment and support of the heart under these circumstances, it is necessary that you be acquainted with some general truths which have a tendency to calm the trembling and doubting soul; and that you be rightly instructed with regard to the above-mentioned causes of disquiet. Let me direct your attention to the following general truths:

1. Every appearance of hypocrisy does not prove the person who manifests it to be a hypocrite. You should carefully distinguish between the appearance and the predominance of hypocrisy. There are remains of deceitfulness in the best hearts; this was exemplified in David and Peter; but the prevailing frame of their hearts being upright, they were not denominated hypocrites for their conduct.

2. We ought to regard what can be said in our favour, as well as what may be said against us. It is the sin of upright persons sometimes, to exercise an unreasonable severity against themselves. They do not impartially consider the state of their souls. To make their state appear better than it really is, indeed is the damning sin of self-flattering hypocrites; and to make their state appear worse than it really is, is the sin and folly of some good persons.

But why should you be such an enemy to your own peace? Why read over the evidences of God's love to your soul, as a man does a book which he intends to confute? Why do you study evasions, and turn off those comforts which are due to you?

3. Every thing which may be an occasion of grief to the people of God, is not a sufficient ground for their questioning the reality of their religion. Many things may trouble, which ought not to stumble you. If upon every occasion you should call in question all that had ever been wrought upon you, your life would be made up of doubtings and fears, and you could never attain that settled inward peace, and live that life of praise and thankfulness which the Gospel requires.

4. The soul is not at all times in a suitable state to pass a right judgment upon itself. It is peculiarly unqualified for this in the hour of desertion or temptation. Such seasons must be improved rather for watching and resisting, than for judging and determining.

5. Whatever be the ground of one's distress, it should drive him to, not from God. Suppose you have sinned thus and so, or that you have been thus long and sadly deserted, yet

you have no right to infer that you ought to be discouraged, as if there was no help for you in God.

When you have well digested these truths, if your doubts and distress remain, consider what is now to be offered:

(i) Are you ready to conclude that you have no part in the favour of God, because you are visited with some extraordinary affliction? If so, do you then rightly conclude that great trials are tokens of God's hatred? Does the Scripture teach this? And dare you infer the same with respect to all who have been as much or more afflicted than yourself? If the argument is good in your case, it is good in application to theirs, and more conclusive with respect to them, in proportion as their trials were greater than yours. Woe then to David, Job, Paul, and all who have been afflicted as they were! But had you passed along in quietness and prosperity; had God withheld those chastisements with which he ordinarily visits his people, would you not have far more reason for doubts and distress than you now have?

(ii) Do you rashly infer that the Lord has no love to you, because he has withdrawn the light of his countenance? Do you imagine your state to be hopeless, because it is dark and uncomfortable? Be not hasty in forming this conclusion. If any of the dispensations of God to his people will bear a favourable as well as a harsh construction, why should they not be construed in the best sense? And may not God have a design of love rather than of hatred in the dispensation under which you mourn? May he not depart for a season, without departing for ever? You are not the first that have mistaken the design of God in withdrawing himself. 'Zion said, The Lord hath forsaken me, my Lord hath forgotten me.' But was it so? What saith the answer of God? 'Can a woman forget her sucking child?'

But do you sink down under the apprehension that the evidences of a total and final desertion are discoverable in your experience? Have you then lost your conscientious tenderness with regard to sin? And are you inclined to forsake God? If so, you have reason indeed to be alarmed. But if your conscience is tenderly alive; if you are resolved to cleave to the Lord; if the language of your heart is, I cannot forsake God, I cannot live without his presence; though he slay me, yet will I trust in him: then you have reason to hope that he will visit you again. It is by these exercises that he still maintains his interest in you.

Once more. Are sense and feelings suitable to judge of the dispensations of God by? Can their testimony be safely relied on? Is it safe to argue thus: 'If God had any love for my soul, I should feel it now as well as in former times; but I cannot feel it, therefore it is gone?' May you not as well conclude, when the sun is invisible to you, that he has ceased to exist? Read Isaiah 1:10.

Now if there is nothing in the divine dealings with you which is a reasonable ground of your despondency and distress, let us inquire what there is in your own conduct for which you should be so cast down:

(i) Have you committed sins from which you were formerly recovered with shame and sorrow? And do you thence conclude that you sin allowedly and habitually, and that your oppositions to sin were hypocritical? But do not too hastily give up all for lost. Is not your repentance and care renewed as often as you commit sin? Is it not the sin itself which troubles you, and is it not true, that the oftener you sin the more you are distressed? It is not so in customary sinning; of which Bernard excellently discourses thus: 'When a man accustomed to restrain, sins grievously, it seems insupportable to him, yea he seems to descend alive into hell. In process of time it seems not insupportable, but heavy, and between insupportable and heavy there is no small descent. Next, such sinning becomes light, his conscience smites but faintly, and he regards not her rebukes. Then he is not only insensible to his guilt, but that which was bitter and displeasing has become in some degree sweet and pleasant. Now it is made a custom, and not only pleases, but pleases habitually. At length custom becomes nature; he cannot be dissuaded from it, but defends and pleads for it.' This is allowed and customary sinning, this is the way of the wicked. But is not your way the contrary of this?

(ii) Do you apprehend a decline of your affections from God and from spiritual subjects? This may be your case, and yet there may be hope. But possibly you are mistaken with regard to this. There are many things to be learnt in Christian experience; it has relation to a great variety of subjects. You may now be learning what it is very necessary for you to know as a Christian. Now, what if you are not sensible of so lively affections, of such ravishing views as you had at first; may not your piety be growing more solid and consistent, and better adapted to practical purposes? Does it follow from your not always being in the same frame of mind, or from the fact that the same objects do not at all times excite the same feelings, that you have no true religion? Perhaps you deceive yourself by looking forward to what you would be, rather than contemplating what you are, compared with what you once were.

(iii) If the strength of your love to creature-enjoyments is the ground of desperate conclusions respecting yourself, perhaps you argue thus: 'I fear that I love the creature more than God, if so, I have not true love to God. I sometimes feel stronger affections toward earthly comforts than I do toward heavenly objects, therefore my soul is not upright within me.' If, indeed, you love the creature for itself, if you make it your end, and religion but a means, then you conclude rightly; for this is incompatible with supreme love to God. But may not a man love God more ardently and unchangeably than he does any thing, or all things else, and yet, when God is not the direct object of his thoughts, may he not be sensible of more violent affection for the creature than he has at that time for God? As rooted malice indicates a stronger hatred than sudden though more violent passion, so we must judge of our love, not by a violent motion of it now and then, but by the depth of its root and the constancy of its exercise. Perhaps your difficulty results from bringing your love to some foreign and improper test. Many persons have feared that when brought to some eminent trial they should renounce Christ and cleave to the creature; but when the trial came, Christ was everything, and the world as nothing in their esteem. Such were the fears of some martyrs whose victory was complete. But you may expect divine assistance only at the time of, and in proportion to your necessity. If you would try your love, see whether you are willing to forsake Christ now.

(iv) Is the want of that enlargement in private which you find in public exercises an occasion of doubts and fears? Consider then whether there are not some circumstances attending public duties which are peculiarly calculated to excite your feelings and elevate your mind, and which cannot affect you in private. If so, your exercises in secret, if performed faithfully and in a suitable manner, may be profitable, though they have not all the characteristics of those in public. If you imagine that you have spiritual enlargement and enjoyment in public exercises while you neglect private duties, doubtless you deceive yourself. Indeed *if you live in the neglect of secret duties, or are careless about them, you have great reason to fear.* But if you regularly and faithfully perform them, it does not follow that they are vain and worthless, or that they are not of great value, because they are not attended with so much enlargement as you sometimes find in public. And what if the Spirit is pleased more highly to favour you with his gracious influence in one place and at one time than another, should this be a reason for murmuring and unbelief, or for thankfulness?

(v) The vile or blasphemous suggestions of Satan sometimes occasion great perplexity and distress. They seem to lay open an abyss of corruption in the heart, and to say there can be no grace here. But there may be grace in the heart where such thoughts are injected, though not in the heart which consents to and cherishes them. Do you then abhor and oppose them? Do you utterly refuse to give up yourself to their influence, and strive to keep holy and reverend thoughts of God, and of all religious objects? If so, such suggestions are involuntary, and no evidence against your piety.

(vi) Is the seeming denial of your prayers an occasion of despondency? Are you disposed to say, 'If God had any regard for my soul he would have heard my petitions before now; but I have no answer from him, and therefore no interest in him'? But stay: though God's abhorring and finally rejecting prayer is an evidence that he rejects the person who prays, yet, dare you conclude that he has rejected you, because an answer to your prayers is delayed, or because you do not discover it if granted? 'May not God bear long with his own elect, that cry unto him day and night?'

Others have stumbled upon the same ground with you: 'I said in my haste, I am cut off from before thine eyes: nevertheless thou heardst the voice of my supplication.' Now are there not some things in your experience which indicate that your prayers are not rejected, though answer to them is deferred? Are you not disposed to continue praying though you do not discover an answer? Are you not disposed still to ascribe righteousness to God, while you consider the cause of his silence as being in yourself? Thus did David: 'O my God, I cry in the day time, and thou hearest not; and in the night, and am not silent: but thou art holy.' Does not the delay of an answer to your prayers excite you to examine your own heart and try your ways, that you may find and remove the difficulty? If so, you have reason for humiliation, but not for despair.

Thus I have shown you how to keep your heart in dark and doubting seasons. God forbid that any false heart should encourage itself from these things. It is lamentable, that when we give saints and sinners their proper portions, each is so prone to take up the other's part.

Another season, wherein the heart must be kept with all diligence, is *when sufferings for religion are laid upon us.* Blessed is the man who in such a season is not offended in Christ. Now, whatever may be the kind or degree of your sufferings, if they are sufferings for Christ's sake and the Gospel's, spare no diligence to keep your heart. If you are tempted to shrink or waver under them, let what follows help you to repel and to surmount the instigation:

1. What reproach would you cast upon the Redeemer and his religion by deserting him at such a time as this! You would proclaim to the world, that how much soever you

have boasted of the promises, when you are put to the proof you dare hazard nothing upon your faith in them; and this will give the enemies of Christ an occasion to blaspheme. And will you thus furnish the triumphs of the uncircumcised? Ah, if you did but value the name of Christ as much as many wicked men value their names, you could never endure that his should be exposed to contempt. Will proud dust and ashes hazard death or hell rather than have their names disgraced, and will you endure nothing to maintain the honour of Christ?

2. Dare you violate your conscience out of complaisance to flesh and blood? Who will comfort you when your conscience accuses and condemns you? What happiness can there be in life, liberty or friends, when inward peace is taken away? Consider well what you do.

3. Is not the public interest of Christ and his cause infinitely more important than any interest of your own, and should you not prefer his glory and the welfare of his kingdom before everything else? Should any temporary suffering, or any sacrifice which you can be called to make, be suffered to come into competition with the honour of his name?

4. Did the Redeemer neglect your interest and think lightly of you, when for your sake he endured sufferings between which and yours there can be no comparison? Did he hesitate and shrink back? No: 'He endured the cross, despising the shame.' And did he with unbroken patience and constancy endure so much for you; and will you flinch from momentary suffering in his cause?

5. Can you so easily cast off the society and the privileges of the saints and go over to the enemy's side? Are you willing

to withhold your support from those who are determined to preserve, and throw your influence in the scale against them? Rather let your body and soul be rent asunder. 'If any man draw back, my soul shall have no pleasure in him.'

6. How can you stand before Christ in the day of judgment, if you desert him now? 'He that is ashamed of me and of my words in this adulterous and sinful generation, of him shall the Son of man be ashamed when he cometh in the glory of his Father with the holy angels.' Yet a little while, and the Son of man will come in the clouds of heaven, with power and great glory, to judge the world. He will sit upon the throne of judgment, while all the nations are brought before him. Imagine yourself now to be witnessing the transactions of that day. Behold the wicked; behold the apostates; and hear the consuming sentence which is pronounced upon them, and see them sinking in the gulf of infinite and everlasting woe! And will you desert Christ now, will you forsake his cause to save a little suffering, or to protract an unprofitable life on earth, and thus expose yourself to the doom of the apostate? Remember, that if you can silence the remonstrances of conscience now, you cannot hinder the sentence of the Judge then. By these means *keep your heart, that it depart not from the living God.*

The last season which I shall mention, in which the heart must be kept with all diligence, is *when we are warned by sickness that our dissolution is at hand.* When the child of God draws nigh to eternity, the adversary makes his last effort; and as he cannot win the soul from God, as he cannot dissolve the bond which unites the soul to Christ, his great design is to awaken fears of death, to fill the mind with aversion and horror at the thoughts of dissolution from the body. Hence, what shrinking from a separation, what fear to grasp death's cold hand, and unwillingness to depart, may sometimes be observed in the people of God. But we ought to die, as well as live, like saints.

I shall offer several considerations calculated to help the people of God in time of sickness, to keep their hearts loose from all earthly objects, and cheerfully willing to die:

1. Death is harmless to the people of God; its shafts leave no sting in them. Why then are you afraid that your sickness may be unto death? If you were to die in your sins; if death were to reign over you as a tyrant, to feed upon you as a lion doth upon his prey; if death to you were to be the precursor of hell, then you might reasonably startle and shrink back from it with horror and dismay. But if your sins are blotted out; if Christ has vanquished death in your behalf, so that you have nothing to encounter but bodily pain, and possibly not even that; if death will be to you the harbinger of heaven, why should you be afraid? Why not bid it welcome? It cannot hurt you; it is easy and harmless; it is like putting off your clothes, or taking rest.

2. It may keep your heart from shrinking back, to consider that death is necessary to fit you for the full enjoyment of God. Whether you are willing to die or not, there certainly is no other way to complete the happiness of your soul. Death must do you the kind office to remove this veil of flesh, this animal life which separates you from God, before you can see and enjoy him fully. 'Whilst we are at home in the body, we are absent from the Lord.' And who would not be willing to die for the perfect enjoyment of God? Methinks one should look and sigh, like a prisoner, through the grates of this mortality: 'O that I had wings like a dove,

then would I fly away and be at rest.' Indeed most men need patience to die; but a saint, who understands what death will introduce him to, rather needs patience to live. On his death-bed he should often look out and listen to his Lord's coming; and when he perceives his dissolution to be near, he should say, 'The voice of my beloved; behold he cometh, leaping over the mountains, skipping over the hills.'

3. Consider that the happiness of heaven commences immediately after death. *That* happiness will not be deferred till the resurrection; but as soon as death has passed upon you, your soul will be swallowed up in life. When you have once loosed from this shore, you shall be quickly wafted to the shore of a glorious eternity. And can you not say, *I desire to be dissolved, and to be with Christ?* Did the soul and body die together, or did they sleep till the resurrection, as some have fancied, it would have been folly for Paul to desire a dissolution for the enjoyment of Christ; because he would have enjoyed more in the body than he could have enjoyed out of it.

The Scripture speaks of but two ways in which the soul can properly live: viz. by *faith* and *vision*. These two comprehend its present and future existence. Now, if when faith fails, sight should not immediately succeed, what would become of soul? But the truth on this subject is clearly revealed in Scripture. See Luke 23:43, John 14:3. What a blessed change then will death make in your condition! Rouse up, dying saint, and rejoice; let death do his work, that the angels may conduct your soul to the world of light.

4. It may increase your willingness to die, to reflect that by death God often removes his people out of the way of great troubles and temptations. When some extraordinary

calamity is coming upon the world, God sometimes removes his saints out of the way of the evil. Thus Methuselah died the year before the flood; Augustine a little before the sacking of Hippo; Pareus just before the taking of Heidelburg. Luther observes that all the apostles died before the destruction of Jerusalem; and Luther himself died before the wars broke out in Germany. Now it may be that by death you will escape some grievous trial, which you could not and need not endure. But if no extraordinary trouble would come upon you in case your life were prolonged, yet God designs by death to relieve you from innumerable evils and burdens which are inseparable from the present state. Thus you will be delivered from indwelling sin, which is the greatest trouble; from all temptations from whatever source; from bodily tempers and embarrassments; and from all the afflictions and sorrows in this life. The days of your mourning will be ended, and God will wipe away all tears from your eyes. Why then should you not hasten to depart?

5. If you still linger, like Lot in Sodom, what are your pleas and pretences for a longer life? Why are you unwilling to die? Are you concerned for the welfare of your relations? If so, are you anxious for their temporal support? Then let the word of God satisfy you: 'Leave thy fatherless children to me, I will keep them alive, and let thy widows trust in me.' Luther says, in his last will, 'Lord, thou hast given me a wife and children, I have nothing to leave them, but I commit them unto thee. Oh Father of the fatherless and Judge of widows, nourish, keep and teach them.'

But are you concerned for the spiritual welfare of your relations? Remember that you cannot convert them, if you should live; and God can make your prayers and counsels effectual when you are dead.

Perhaps you desire to serve God longer in this world. But if he has nothing further for you to do here, why not say with David, 'Here am I, let him do what seemeth him good.' He is calling you to higher service in heaven, and can accomplish by other hands what you desire to do further here. Do you feel too imperfect to go to heaven? Consider that you must be imperfect until you die; your sanctification cannot be complete until you get to heaven.

'But,' you say, 'I want assurance; if I had that I could die easily.' Consider, then, that a hearty willingness to leave all the world to be freed from sin, and to be with God, is the direct way to that desired assurance; no carnal person was ever willing to die upon this ground.

Thus I have shown how the people of God, in the most difficult seasons, may keep their hearts with all diligence.

4

Improving and Applying the Subject

1. You have seen that the keeping of the heart is the great work of a Christian, in which the very soul and life of religion consists, and without which all other duties are of no value in the sight of God. Hence, to the consternation of hypocrites and formal professors, I infer:

(i) That the pains and labours which many persons have undergone in religion are of no value, and will turn to no good account. Many splendid services have been performed by men, which God will utterly reject: they will not stand on record in order to an eternal acceptance, because the performers took no heed to keep their hearts with God. This is that fatal rock on which thousands of vain professors dash and ruin themselves eternally; they are exact about the externals of religion, but regardless of their hearts. O how many hours have some professors spent in hearing, praying, reading and conferring! and yet, as to the main end of religion, they might as well have sat still and done nothing, the great work, I mean heart-work, being all the while neglected. Tell me, vain professor, when did you shed a tear for the deadness, hardness, unbelief or earthliness of your heart? And do you think your easy religion can save you? If so, you must invert Christ's words, and say, *Wide is the gate and broad is the way that leadeth to life, and many there be that go in thereat!* Hear me, ye self-deluding hypocrite; you who have put off God with heartless duties; you who have acted in religion as if you had been blessing an idol; you who could not search your heart, and regulate it, and exercise it in your performances; how will you abide the coming of the Lord? How will you hold up your head before him, when he shall say 'O you dissembling, false-hearted man! how could you profess religion? With what face could you so often tell me that you loved me, when you knew in your conscience that your heart was not with me?' O tremble to think what a fearful judgment it is to be given over to a heedless and careless heart, and then to have religious duties instead of a rattle to quiet and still the conscience!

(ii) I infer for their humiliation, that unless the *people of God* spend more time and pains about their hearts than they ordinarily do, they are never like to do God much service, or to possess much comfort in this world. I may say of that Christian who is remiss and careless in keeping his heart, as Jacob said of Reuben, *Thou shalt not excel.* It grieves me to see how many Christians there are who live at a poor, low rate, both of service and comfort, and who go up and down dejecting and complaining. But how can they expect it should be otherwise, while they live so carelessly? O how little of their time is spent in the closet, in searching, humbling, and quickening their hearts!

Christian, you say your heart is dead, and do you wonder that it is, so long as you keep it not with the fountain of life? If your body had been dieted as your soul has, that would have been dead too. And you may never expect that your heart will be in a better state until you take more pains with it.

O Christians! I fear your zeal and strength have run in the wrong channel; I fear that most of us may take up the Church's complaint: 'They have made me the keeper of the vineyards, but mine own vineyard have I not kept.' Two things have eaten up the time and strength of the professors of this generation, and sadly diverted them from heart-work.

First, fruitless controversies, started by Satan, I doubt not for the very purpose of taking us off from practical godliness, to make us puzzle our heads when we should be inspecting our hearts. How little have we regarded the observation: 'It is a good thing that the heart be established with grace, and not with meats' (that is, with disputes and controversies about meats) 'which have not profited them that have been occupied therein.' How much better it is to see men live exactly, than to hear them dispute with subtlety! These unfruitful questions, how have they rent the churches, wasted time and spirits, and taken Christians off from their main business!

What think you, would it not have been better if the questions agitated among the people of God of late had been such as these: 'How shall a man distinguish the special from the common operations of the Spirit? How may a soul discern its first backslidings from God? How may a backsliding Christian recover his first love? How may the heart be preserved from unseasonable thoughts in duty? How may a bosom-sin be discovered and mortified?'

Would not this course have tended more to the honour of religion and the comfort of souls? I am ashamed that the professors of this generation are yet insensible of their folly. Oh that God would turn their disputes and contentions into practical godliness!

Second, worldly cares and encumbrances have greatly increased the neglect of our hearts. The heads and hearts of multitudes have been filled with such a crowd and noise of worldly business that they have lamentably declined in their zeal, their love, their delight in God, and their heavenly, serious, and profitable way of conversing with men. How miserably have we entangled ourselves in this wilderness of trifles! Our discourses, our conferences, nay, our very prayers are tinged with it. We have had so much to do without, that we have been able to do but little within. And how many precious opportunities have we thus lost? How many admonitions of the Spirit have passed over unfruitfully? How often has the Lord called to us, when our worldly thoughts have prevented us from hearing? But there certainly is a way to enjoy God even in our worldly employments. If we lose our views of him when engaged in our temporal affairs, the fault is our own. Alas! that Christians should stand at the door of eternity, having more work upon their hands than their time is sufficient for, and yet be filling their heads and hearts with trifles!

(iii) I infer, lastly, for the awakening of all, that if the keeping of the heart be the great work of a Christian, then there are but few real Christians in the world. If every one who has learned the dialect of Christianity, and who can talk like a saint; if every one who has gifts and parts, and who can make shift to preach, pray, or discourse like a Christian: in a word, if all such as associate with the people of

God and partake of ordinances may pass for Christians, then indeed the number is great. But alas! how few can be found, if you judge them by this rule – how few are there who conscientiously keep their hearts, watch their thoughts and look scrupulously to their motives! Indeed there are few *closet-men* among professors.

It is easier for men to be reconciled to any other duties in religion than to these. The profane part of the world will not so much as meddle with the outside of any religious duties, and least of all with these; and as to the hypocrite, though he may be very particular in externals, you can never persuade him to undertake this inward, this difficult work; this work, to which there is no inducement from human applause; this work, which would quickly discover what the hypocrite cares not to know: so that by general consent this heart-work is left to the hands of a few retired ones, and I tremble to think in how few hands it is.

2. If the keeping of the heart be so important a business; if such great advantages result from it; if so many valuable interests be wrapt up in it, then let me call upon the people of God everywhere to engage heartily in this work. Study your hearts, watch your hearts, keep your hearts! Away with fruitless controversies and all idle questions; away with empty names and vain shows; away with unprofitable discourse and bold censures of others, and turn in upon yourselves. O that this day, this hour, you would resolve upon doing so!

Reader, methinks I shall prevail with you. All that I beg for is this, that you would step aside oftener to talk with God and your own heart; that you would not suffer every trifle to divert you; that you would keep a more true and faithful account of your thoughts and affections; that you would seriously demand of your own heart at least every evening, 'O my heart, where hast thou been today, and what has engaged thy thoughts?'

If all that has been said by way of inducement be not enough, I have yet some motives to offer you:

(i) The studying, observing, and diligently keeping your own heart, will surprisingly help you to understand the deep mysteries of religion. An honest, well-experienced heart is an excellent help to the head. Such a heart will serve for a commentary on a great part of the Scriptures. By means of such a heart you will have a better understanding of divine things than the most learned (graceless) man ever had, or can have; you will not only have a clearer, but a more interesting and profitable apprehension of them. A man may discourse orthodoxly and profoundly of the nature and effects of faith, the troubles and comforts of conscience, and the sweetness of communion with God, who never felt the efficacy and sweet impression of these things upon his own soul. But how dark and dry are his notions compared with those of an experienced Christian!

(ii) The study and observation of your own heart will powerfully secure you against the dangerous and infecting errors of the times in which you live. For what think you is the reason why so many professors have departed from the faith, giving heed to fables? Why have so many been led away by the error of the wicked? Why have those who have sown corrupt doctrines had such plentiful harvests among us, but because they have met with a race of professors who never knew what belongs to practical godliness and the study and keeping of their hearts?

(iii) Your care and diligence in keeping your heart will prove one of the best evidences of your sincerity. I know no external act of religion which truly distinguishes the sound from the unsound professor. It is marvellous how far hypocrites go in all external duties; how plausibly they can order the outward man, hiding all their indecencies from the observation of the world. But they take no heed to their hearts; they are not in secret what they appear to be in public; and before this test no hypocrite can stand. They may, indeed, in a fit of terror, or on a death-bed, cry out of the wickedness of their hearts; but such extorted complaints are worthy of no regard. No credit, in law, is to be given to the testimony of one upon the rack, because it may be supposed that the extremity of his torture will make him say any thing to get relief. But if self-jealousy, care and watchfulness be the daily workings and frames of your heart, you have some evidence of your sincerity.

(iv) How comfortable and how profitable would all ordinances and duties be to you, if your heart was faithfully kept. What lively communion might you have with God every time you approach him, if your heart was in a right frame! You might then say with David, 'My meditation of him shall be sweet.' It is the indisposition of the heart which renders ordinances, and secret duties so comfortless to some. They strive to raise their hearts to God, now pressing this argument upon them, then that, to quicken and affect them; yet they often get nearly through the exercise before their hearts begin to be interested in it; and sometimes they go away no better than they came. But the Christian whose heart is prepared by being constantly kept, enters immediately and heartily into his duties; he outstrips his sluggish neighbour, gets the first sight of Christ in a sermon, the first seal from Christ in a sacrament, the first communication of grace and love in secret prayer. Now if there be anything valuable and comfortable in ordinances and private duties, look to your heart and keep it, I beseech you.

(v) An acquaintance with your own heart will furnish you a fountain of matter in prayer. The man who is diligent in heart-work will be richly supplied with matter in his addresses to God. He will not be confused for want of thoughts; his tongue will not falter for want of expressions.

(vi) The most desirable thing in the world, viz. the revival of religion among a people, may be effected by means of what I am urging upon you.

O that I might see the time when professors shall not walk in a vain show; when they shall please themselves no more with a name to live, while they are spiritually dead; when they shall be no more a company of frothy, vain persons; but when holiness shall shine in their conversation, and awe the world, and command reverence from all that are around them; when they shall warm the heart of those who come near them, and cause it to be said, God is in these men of a truth. And may such a time be expected? Until heart-work becomes the business of professors, I have no hope of seeing a time so blessed! Does it not grieve you to see how religion is contemned and trampled under foot, and the professors of it ridiculed and scorned in the world? Professors, would you recover your credit? Would you obtain an honourable testimony in the consciences of your very enemies? Then keep your hearts.

(vii) By diligence in keeping our hearts we should prevent the occasions of fatal scandals and stumbling-blocks to the world. Woe to the world because of offences!

Keep your heart faithfully, and you will be prepared for any situation or service to which you may be called. This, and this only can properly fit you for usefulness in any station; but with this you can endure prosperity or adversity; you can deny yourself, and turn your hand to any work. Thus Paul turned every circumstance to good account, and made himself so eminently useful. When he preached to others, he provided against being cast away himself: he kept his heart; and everything in which he excelled seems to have had a close connection with his diligence in keeping his heart.

(viii) If the people of God would diligently keep their hearts, their communion with each other would be unspeakably more inviting and profitable. Then 'how goodly would be thy tents, O Jacob, and thy tabernacles, O Israel!' It is the fellowship which the people of God have with the Father and with the Son that kindles the desires of others to have communion with them. I tell you, that if saints would be persuaded to spend more time and take more pains about their hearts, there would soon be such a divine excellence in their conversation that others would account it no small privilege to be with or near them. It is the pride, passion and earthliness of our hearts, that has spoiled Christian fellowship. Why is it that when Christians meet they are often jarring and contending, but because their passions are unmortified? Whence come their uncharitable censures of their brethren, but from their ignorance of themselves? Why is their discourse so light and unprofitable when they meet, but because their hearts are earthly and vain? But now, if Christians would study their hearts more and keep them better, the beauty and glory of communion would be restored. They would divide no more, contend no more, censure rashly no more. They will feel right one toward another, when each is daily humbled under a sense of the evil of his own heart.

(ix) Lastly: Keep your heart, and then the comforts of the Spirit and the influence of all ordinances will be more fixed and lasting than they now are. 'And do the consolations of God seem small to you?' Ah, you have reason to be ashamed that the ordinances of God, as to their quickening and comforting effects, should make so light and transient an impression on your heart.

Now, reader, consider well these special benefits of keeping the heart which I have mentioned. Examine their importance. Are they small matters? Is it a small matter to have your understanding assisted? Your endangered soul rendered safe? Your sincerity proved? Your communion with God sweetened? Your heart filled with matter for prayer? Is it a small thing to have the power of godliness? all fatal scandals removed? an instrumental fitness to serve Christ obtained? the communion of saints restored to its primitive glory? and the influence of ordinances abiding in the souls of saints? If these are no common blessings, no ordinary benefits, then surely it is a great and indispensable duty to keep the heart with all diligence.

And now are you inclined to undertake the business of keeping your heart? Are you resolved upon it? I charge you, then, to engage in it earnestly. Away with every cowardly feeling, and make up your mind to encounter difficulties.

Draw your armour from the word of God. Let the word of Christ dwell in you richly, in its commands, its promises, its threatenings; let it be fixed in your understanding, your memory, your conscience, your affections. You must learn to wield the sword of the Spirit (which is the word of God) familiarly, if you would defend your heart and conquer your enemies.

You must call yourself frequently to an account; examine yourself as in the presence of the all-seeing God; bring your conscience, as it were, to the bar of judgment.

Beware how you plunge yourself into a multiplicity of worldly business; how you practise upon the maxims of the world; and how you venture at all to indulge your depraved propensities.

You must exercise the utmost vigilance to discover and check the first symptoms of departure from God, the least decline of spirituality, or the least indisposition to meditation by yourself, and holy conversation and fellowship with others.

These things you must undertake, in the strength of Christ, with invincible resolution in the outset. And if you thus engage in this great work, be assured you shall not spend your strength for naught; comforts which you never felt or thought of will flow in upon you from every side. The diligent prosecution of this work will constantly afford you the most powerful excitements to vigilance and ardour in the life of faith, while it increases your strength and wears out your enemies.

And when you have kept your heart with all diligence a little while; when you have fought the battles of this spiritual warfare, gained the ascendancy over the corruptions within, and vanquished the enemies without, then God will open the gate of heaven to you, and give you the portion which is promised to them that overcome.

Awake then, this moment; get the world under your feet, pant not for the things which a man may have, and eternally lose his soul; but bless God that you may have his service here, and the glory hereafter which he appoints to his chosen.

'Now the God of peace, that brought again from the dead our Lord Jesus, that great Shepherd of the sheep, through the blood of the everlasting covenant, make you perfect in every good work to do his will, working in you that which is well pleasing in his sight, through Jesus Christ; to whom be glory for ever and ever. Amen.'

Also available in this series....

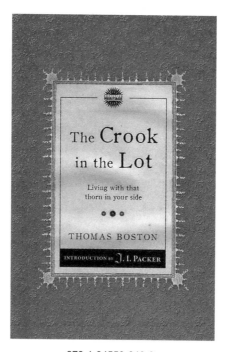

The Crook
in the Lot

Living with that
thorn in your side

● ● ●

THOMAS BOSTON

INTRODUCTION BY J. I. PACKER

978-1-84550-649-0

The Crook in the Lot

A Puritan's Understanding of that Thorn in your side

THOMAS BOSTON

'…the pure biblical wisdom of The Crook in the Lot is badly needed by many of us, and so I am delighted that it is being made available again in this handy form'

J. I. Packer

First published in 1737 this book holds a special place among the tremendous amount of Puritan literature that was produced during that time. Thomas Boston was renowned for his clearly understood English and the manner in which he maintained that clarity while conveying messages of great depth.

The Crook in the Lot is introduced to us by J. I. Packer. In an extensive prologue he shows how Boston's advice remains deeply relevant today. Boston was not preaching merely from his theological understanding, he was speaking from direct personal experience. Boston had real 'thorns' to deal with himself, ranging from his wife's paralyzing depression to his own experiences living for years with what were probably kidney stones. He brings his own unique combination of wonderfully profound and yet immensely practical advice to bear to give us a work of lasting impact.

The
Pleasantness
of a
Religious Life

Life as good as it can be

MATTHEW HENRY

INTRODUCTION BY J. I. PACKER

978-1-84550-651-3

The Pleasantness of a Religious Life

A Puritan's View of the good life

MATTHEW HENRY

'Here is a bait that has no hook under it…a pleasure which God himself invites you to, and which will make you happy, truly and eternally happy…it is certain that there is true pleasure in true religion.'

Matthew Henry

Matthew Henry, the great Puritan commentator, here looks at what gives people real joy. He looks at twelve different types of Christian pleasure, reviews what God has done to bring sinners joy, demonstrates that Christian experience proves this and challenges the reader to join in!

This was Matthew Henry's last book and was at the press when he died in 1714.

This classic of Christian living is brought to you by J. I. Packer who adds an extensive introduction to the book showing its significance and gestation from Henry's ministry.

'We too get told that being a Christian is a bleak and burdensome business, and not being a Christian could be more fun; we too, like Henry's first hearers and readers, need to be reminded that it is absolutely not so.'

THE PURITAN PORTRAITS SERIES

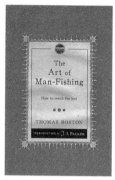

978-1-78191-108-2

978-1-84550-976-7

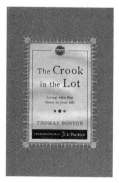

978-1-84550-649-0

978-1-84550-650-6

978-1-84550-648-3

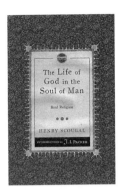

978-1-78191-107-5

978-1-84550-977-4

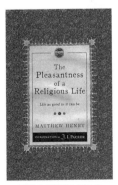

978-1-84550-651-3

978-1-84550-975-0

TRUTHFORLIFE®

Truth For Life is the Bible-teaching ministry of Alistair Begg. Our mission is to teach the Bible with clarity and relevance so that unbelievers will be converted, believers will be established, and local churches will be strengthened.

Since 1995, Truth For Life has aired a Bible-teaching broadcast on the radio, which is now distributed on 1,628 radio outlets each day, and freely on podcast and on the Truth For Life mobile app. Additionally, a large content archive of full-length Bible-teaching sermons is available for free download at www.truthforlife.org.

Truth For Life also makes full-length Bible-teaching available on CD and DVD. These materials, and also books authored by Alistair Begg, are made available at cost, with no markup, so that price is not a barrier to those seeking a deeper understanding of God's Word.

The ministry connects with listeners at live listener and pastor events and conferences across the U.S. and Canada in cities where the radio program is heard.

Contact Truth For Life

In the U.S.:
PO Box 398000, Cleveland, OH 44139, 1.888.588.7884

www.truthforlife.org   letters@truthforlife.org

In Canada:
P.O. Box 19008, Delta, BC V4L 2P8, 1.877.518.7884

www.truthforlife.ca   letters@truthforlife.ca

And also at:

www.facebook.com/truthforlife   www.twitter.com/truthforlife

Christian Focus Publications

Our mission statement –

STAYING FAITHFUL

In dependence upon God we seek to impact the world through literature faithful to His infallible Word, the Bible. Our aim is to ensure that the Lord Jesus Christ is presented as the only hope to obtain forgiveness of sin, live a useful life and look forward to heaven with Him.

Our Books are published in four imprints:

CHRISTIAN
FOCUS

popular works including biographies, commentaries, basic doctrine and Christian living.

CHRISTIAN
HERITAGE

books representing some of the best material from the rich heritage of the church.

MENTOR

books written at a level suitable for Bible College and seminary students, pastors, and other serious readers. The imprint includes commentaries, doctrinal studies, examination of current issues and church history.

CF4·K

children's books for quality Bible teaching and for all age groups: Sunday school curriculum, puzzle and activity books; personal and family devotional titles, biographies and inspirational stories – Because you are never too young to know Jesus!

Christian Focus Publications Ltd,
Geanies House, Fearn, Ross-shire,
IV20 1TW, Scotland, United Kingdom.
www.christianfocus.com